CONCILIUM

Theology in the Age of Renewal

CONCILIUM

Theology in the Age of Renewal

EDITORIAL DIRECTORS: Edward Schillebeeckx (Dogma) •
Herman Schmidt (Liturgy) • Alois Müller (Pastoral) •
Hans Küng (Ecumenism) • Franz Böckle (Moral Theology) •
Johannes B. Metz (Church and World) • Roger Aubert (Church
History) • ✠Néophytos Edelby and Teodoro Jiménez Urresti
(Canon Law) • Christian Duquoc (Spirituality) • Pierre Benoit and
Roland Murphy (Scripture)

CONSULTING EDITORS: Marie-Dominique Chenu • ✠Carlo
Colombo • Yves Congar • Andrew Greeley • Jorge Mejía •
Karl Rahner • Roberto Tucci

EXECUTIVE SECRETARY: (Awaiting new appointment),
Arkstreestraat 3–5, Nijmegen, The Netherlands

Volume 56: Moral Theology

EDITORIAL BOARD: Johannes Baptist Metz •
Willi Oelmüller • Werner Bröker • Alfonso Alvarez Bolado •
Jos Arntz • Paul Blanquart • Henri Bouillard • Daniel Callahan •
Bertrand de Clercq • Joseph Comblin • Etienne Cornélis •
Adolf Darlap • Heimo Dolch • Albert Dondeyne • Dominique
Dubarle • Iring Fetscher • Heinrich Fries • Giulio Girardi •
Jean-Yves Jolif • Andreas van Melsen • Charles Moeller •
Christopher Mooney • Maurice Nédoncelle • Francis O'Farrell •
Raymond Panikkar • Norbert Schiffers • Heinz Schlette •
Alexander Schwan • Juan Segundo • Robert Spaemann •
David Tracy • Josef Trütsch • Roberto Tucci • Jan Walgrave •
Bernhard Welte

MORAL EVIL
UNDER CHALLENGE

Edited by
Johannes B. Metz

Herder and Herder

1970
HERDER AND HERDER
232 Madison Avenue, New York 10016

CONTENTS

PART III

DOCUMENTATION CONCILIUM

Editorial

THE radical way in which moral evil is today being queried or disputed constitutes a challenge to the Christian faith. This number is therefore meant as a contribution to the study of moral evil at the level of the individual, society, and politics.

It deals with a genuine borderline issue of theology which has become a fundamental issue for the contemporary understanding of the faith, in other words, a theme that belongs to fundamental theology.

Philosophers and scientists, particularly since Feuerbach, Marx, Nietzsche and Freud, believe that they have at last disposed of the problem of evil and guilt. Attempts continue to be made to reduce the reality of moral evil and the authenticity of the experience of guilt to a matter of converging psychopathological motivations within the context of social evolution, biological behaviour patterns, and so on.

All this is bound to have some effect on the experience and practice of the faith among believers. A relative (in the sense of not absolute) interpretation of the guilt experience, which has been part of the Christian faith from the beginning, seems to be spreading. In theology and preaching it is becoming increasingly difficult to speak intelligibly and convincingly about moral evil and guilt on traditional lines. We have here, therefore, a fundamental problem of the justification of our faith, which implies the teaching of redemption and reconciliation at its very heart.

As the articles and bulletins show, there are very varying reasons that today lead to this questioning of evil and guilt. Traditional theology has no doubt itself contributed to this underrating and neutralizing of the problem of evil as a non-problem—the personification of evil, the inadequate distinction between physical evil and moral evil, the glib treatment of theodicy and its problems, the one-sided interpretation of original sin and concupiscence, and so on. Unfortunately, there was no time to include an article which would show how these points contributed to the way in which evil and guilt are at present being approached.

In the first article Ricoeur has tried to establish some basic points about the ethical and religious aspect of guilt, based on a semantic analysis of the word "guilt".

Since the theme seemed to require as much information as possible, this issue contains a greater number of *bulletins*. These will provide information about specific interpretations and aspects of the problem of evil and guilt: the philosophical theories about evil, particularly since Kant (Post), the problem of moral decisions in linguistic analysis, particularly in English-speaking countries (Kerr), the problem of evil and guilt in early Buddhism (Berry), the presentation and interpretation of evil in the films of today (Duhourq).

The *articles* deal with the critical theological interpretation of particular positions taken up in this debate. They assume that today the notion of evil and guilt is above all a matter of inter-disciplinary confrontation. Here the authors are less concerned with a comprehensive treatment of the problem within particular disciplines than with the search for points where various disciplines can possibly converge in order to combine in this search for a solution.

A comparison between the Christian teaching of the situation of man and mankind as marked by original sin and the Marxist theory of self-alienation shows that Christian teaching is more than a matter of economic and social self-alienation (Marsch). Beirnaert deals with the legitimacy and limitations of psycho-analytical interpretations of evil and guilt, whilst Schiffers deals with the legitimacy and limitations of behaviour study in this field. Korff sets out the difficulties implied in a "morality without guilt" in an analysis of the various theories of the "new morality".

After this theological discussion of specific views Pohier explains in a hermeneutical essay how theology and preaching can speak today about moral evil and guilt in view of the varied denials or re-interpretations prevailing in a world dominated by science and technology.

PART I
ARTICLES

PART I

Paul Ricoeur

Guilt, Ethics and Religion

MY principal task will be to determine the distinction between ethical discourse and religious discourse on the question of guilt. These will be the two main divisions of my analysis.

But, before treating these two respective discourses with a view to distinguishing them and understanding their relationship, I suggest that first we come to an agreement about the meaning of the terms in question. Allow me, then, by way of preface, to develop a semantic analysis of the very term guilt.

I. GUILT: SEMANTIC ANALYSIS

I propose, first, to consider this term, not in its psychological, psychiatric or psychoanalytic usage, but in the *texts* where its meaning has been constituted and fixed. These texts are those of penitential literature wherein the believing communities have expressed their avowal of evil; the language of these texts is a specific language which can be designated, in a very general way, as "confession of sins", although no particular confessional connotation is attached to this expression, not even a specifically Jewish or Christian meaning. Some decades ago, Professor Pettazzoni of Rome wrote a collection of works covering the entire field of comparative religions. He called this precisely "Confession of Sins". But it is not from the comparative point of view that I take up the problem. My point of departure is in a *phenomenology of confession* or avowal. Here I understand by phenomenology the description of meanings implied in experience in general, whether that experience be one of things, of values, of persons, etc. A phenomenology of confession is therefore a description of meanings and of signified intentions, present in a certain activity of language: the language of confession. Our task, in the framework of such a phenomenology, is to re-enact in ourselves the confession of evil, in order to uncover its aims. By sympathy and through imagination, the philosopher adopts the motivations and intentions of the confessing consciousness; he does not "feel", he "experiences" in a neutral manner, in the manner of an "as if", that which has been lived in the confessing consciousness.

But with which expressions shall we start? Not with expressions of confessions that are the most developed, the most rationalized, for example, the concept or quasi-concept of "original sin" which has often guided philosophical thought. On the contrary, philosophical reasoning should consult expressions of the confession of evil which are the least elaborated, the least articulated.

We should not be embarrassed by the fact that behind these rationalized expressions, behind these speculations, we encounter myths, that is, traditional narratives which tell of events which happened at the origin of time and which lend the support of language to ritual actions. Today, for us, myths are no longer explanations of reality, but, precisely because they have lost their explanatory pretension, they reveal an exploratory significance; they manifest a symbolic function, that is, a way of expressing indirectly the bond between man and what he considers sacred. Paradoxical as it may seem, myth thus demythologized in its contact with physics, cosmology and scientific history becomes a dimension of modern thought. In its turn, myth refers us to a level of expressions, more fundamental than any narration and any speculation; thus, the narrative of the fall in the Bible draws its signification from an experience of sin rooted in the life of the community: it is the cultural activity and the prophetic call to justice and to "mercy" which provide myth with its substructure of significations.

Therefore, it is to this experience and to its language that we must have recourse; or rather, to this experience *in* its language. For it is the language of confession which elevates to the light of discourse an experience charged with emotion, fear and anguish. Penitential literature manifests a linguistic inventiveness which marks the way for existential outbursts of the consciousness of fault.

Let us, therefore, interrogate this language.

The most remarkable characteristic of this language is that it does not involve expressions which are more primitive than the symbolic expressions to which myth refers. The language of confession is symbolic. Here I understand by symbol a language which designates a thing in an indirect way, by designating another thing which it directly indicates. It is in this way that I speak symbolically of elevated thoughts, low sentiments, clear ideas, the light of understanding, the kingdom of heaven, etc. Therefore, the work of repetition as applied to the expressions of evil is, in essence, the explication, the development of different levels of direct and indirect significations which are intermingled in the same symbol. The most archaic symbolism from which we can start is that of evil conceived as defilement or stain, that is, as a spot which contaminates from the outside. In more elaborated literatures, such as that of the Babylonians and especially of the Hebrews, sin is expressed in different symbolisms, such as to miss the target, to follow a tortuous path, to rebel, to have a stiff neck, to be unfaithful as in adultery, to be deaf, to be lost, to wander, to be empty and hollow, to be inconstant as dust.

This linguistic situation is astonishing; the consciousness of self, so intense in the sentiment of evil, does not, at first, have at its disposal an abstract language, but a very concrete language, on which a spontaneous work of interpretation is performed.

The second remarkable characteristic of this language is that it knows itself as symbolic and that, before any philosophy and theology, it is *en route* towards explication; as I have said elsewhere, the symbol "invites" thought; the myth is on the way towards *logos*. This is true even of the archaic idea of defilement or stain: the idea of a quasi-material something which contaminates from the outside, which harms by means of invisible properties—this idea possesses a symbolic richness, a potential of symbolization, which is attested to by the very survival of this symbol under more and more allegorical forms. We speak even today, in a non-medical sense, of contamination by the spirit of monetary profit, by racism, etc.; we have not completely abandoned the symbolism of the pure and the impure. And this, precisely because the quasi-material representation of stain is already symbolic of something else. From the beginning it has symbolic power. Stain has never literally signified a spot, impurity has never literally signified filth; it is located in the chiaroscuro of a quasi-physical infection and of a quasi-moral indignity. We see this clearly in rites of purification which are never just a simple washing; ablution and lustration are already partial and fictive actions which signify, on the level of body, a total action which addresses itself to the person considered as an undivided whole.

The symbolism of sin such as is found in Babylonian and Hebraic literature, in Greek tragedies or in Orphic writings, is certainly richer than that of stain, from which it is sharply distinguished. To the image of impure contact, it opposes that of a wounded relationship, between God and man, between man and man, between man and himself; but this relation, which will be thought of as a relation only by a philosopher, is symbolically signified by all the means of dramatization offered in daily experience. So, too, the idea of sin is not reduced to the barren idea of the rupture of a relation; it adds to this the idea of a power which dominates man. Thus it maintains a certain affinity and continuity with the symbolism of stain. But this power is also the sign of the emptiness, of the vanity of man, represented by breath and by dust. So the symbol of sin is at one and the same time the symbol of something negative (rupture, estrangement, absence, vanity) and the symbol of something positive (power, possession, captivity, alienation). It is on this symbolic foundation, in this network of images and nascent interpretations that the word guilt should be re-situated.

If we want to respect the proper intention of words, the expression guilt does not cover the whole semantic field of "confession". The idea of guilt represents the extreme form of interiorization which we have seen sketched in the passage from stain to sin. Stain was still external contagion, sin already the rupture of a relation; but this rupture exists even if I do not know it; sin is a real condition, an objective situation; I would venture to say, an ontological dimension of existence.

Guilt, on the contrary, has a distinctly subjective accent: its symbolism is much more interior. It describes the consciousness of being overwhelmed by a burden which crushes. It indicates, further, the bite of a remorse which gnaws from within, in the completely interior brooding on fault. These two metaphors of burden and of biting express well the arrival at the level of existence. The most significant symbolism of guilt is that which is attached to the theme of tribunal; the tribunal is a public institution, but metaphorically transposed into the internal forum it becomes what we call the "moral consciousness". Thus guilt becomes a way of putting oneself before a sort of invisible tribunal which measures the offence, pronounces the condemnation and inflicts the punishment; at the extreme point of interiorization, moral consciousness is a look which watches, judges and condemns; the sentiment of guilt is therefore the consciousness of being inculpated and incriminated by this interior tribunal. It is mingled with the anticipation of the punishment; in short, the *coulpe*, in Latin *culpa*, is self-observation, self-accusation and self-condemnation by a consciousness doubled-back on itself.

This interiorization of guilt gives rise to two series of results: on the one hand, the consciousness of guilt marks a definite progress in relation to what we have described as "sin"; while sin is still a collective reality in which a whole community is implicated, guilt tends to individualize itself. (In Israel, the prophets of the exile are the artisans of this progress [Ezek. 31. 34]; this preaching is a liberating action; at a time when a collective return from exile, comparable to the ancient Exodus from Egypt, appeared impossible, a personal path of conversion opened itself to each one. In ancient Greece, it was the tragic poets who assured the passage from hereditary crime to the guilt of the individual hero, placed alone before his own destiny.) Moreover, in becoming individualized, guilt acquires degrees; to the egalitarian experience of sin is opposed the graduated experience of guilt: man is entirely and radically sinner, but more or less guilty. It is the progress of penal law itself, principally in Greece and Rome, which has an effect here on moral consciousness: the whole of penal law is actually an effort to limit and to gauge the penalty in function of the measure of the fault. The idea of a parallel scale of crimes and sins is interiorized, in its own turn, in favour of the metaphor of the tribunal; moral consciousness becomes itself a graduated consciousness of guilt.

This individualization and this gradation of guilt surely indicate a progress in respect to the collective and unqualified character of sin. We cannot say as much for the other series of results: with guilt there arises indeed a sort of demand which can be called scrupulosity and whose ambiguous character is extremely interesting. A scrupulous consciousness is a delicate consciousness, a precise consciousness enamoured of increasing perfection; it is a consciousness anxious to observe all the commandments, to satisfy the law in all things, without making an exception of any sector of existence, without taking into account exterior obstacles, for example, the persecution of a Prince, and which gives equal importance to little things as to great. But at the same time scrupulosity marks the entrance of moral consciousness into its own pathology; a scrupulous person encloses himself in the inextricable labyrinth of commandments; obligation takes on an enumerative and cumulative character, which contrasts with the simplicity and sobriety of the commandment to love God and man. The scrupulous consciousness never stops adding new commandments. This atomization of the law into a multitude of commandments entails an endless "juridization" of action and a quasi-obsessional ritualization of daily life. The scrupulous person never arrives at satisfying all the commandments, or even any one. At the same time even the notion of obedience is perverted; obedience to a commandment, because it is commanded, becomes more important than love of neighbour, and even love of God; this exactitude in observance is what we call legalism. With it we enter into the hell of guilt, such as St Paul described it: the law itself becomes a source of sin. In giving a knowledge of evil, it excites the desire of transgression, and incites the endless movement of condemnation and punishment. The commandment, says St Paul, "has given life to sin", and thus "hands me over to death" (Rom. 7). Law and sin give birth to one another mutually in a terrible vicious circle, which becomes a mortal circle.

Thus, guilt reveals the malediction of a life under the law. At the limit, when the confidence and tenderness, which are still expressed in the conjugal metaphors of Hosea, disappear, guilt leads to an accusation without accuser, a tribunal without judge, a verdict without author. Guilt has then become that irreversible misfortune described by Kafka: condemnation has become damnation.

A conclusion of this semantic analysis is that guilt does not cover the whole field of the human experience of evil; the study of these symbolic expressions has permitted us to distinguish in them a particular moment of this experience, the most ambiguous moment. On the one hand, guilt expresses the interiorization of the experience of evil, and consequently the promotion of a morally responsible subject—but, on the other hand, it marks the beginning of a specific pathology, wherein scrupulosity marks the point of inversion.

Now the problem is posed: what do ethics and the philosophy of religion make of this ambiguous experience of guilt and of the symbolic language in which it is expressed?

II. Ethical Dimension

In what sense is the problem of evil an ethical problem? In a twofold sense, it seems to me. Or rather, by reason of a double relationship, on the one hand with the question of freedom, and on the other hand with the question of obligation. Evil, freedom, obligation constitute a very complex network, which we shall try to unravel and to order in several stages of reflection. I shall begin and end with freedom, for it is the essential point.

In a first stage of reflection, I say: to affirm freedom is to take upon oneself the origin of evil. By this proposition, I affirm a link between evil and liberty, which is so close that the two terms imply one another mutually. Evil has the meaning of evil because it is the work of freedom. Freedom has the meaning of freedom because it is capable of evil: I both recognize and declare myself to be the author of evil. By that fact, I reject as an alibi the claim that evil exists after the manner of a substance or of a nature, that it has the same status as things which can be observed by an outside spectator. This claim is to be found not only in the metaphysical fantasies, such as those against which Augustine fought—Manicheism and all sorts of ontologies which conceive of evil as a being. This claim can take on a positive appearance, or even a scientific appearance, under the form of psychological or socio-logical determinism. To take upon oneself the origin of evil is to lay aside as a weakness the claim that evil is something, that it is an effect in a world of observable things, whether these things be physical, psychic or social realities. I say: it is I who have acted. *Ego sum qui feci.* There is no evil-being; there is only the evil-done-by-me. To take evil upon oneself is an act of language com-parable to the performative, in this sense, that it is a language which does something, that is to say, that it imputes the act to me.

I said that the relationship was reciprocal; indeed, if freedom qualified evil as a doing, evil is that which reveals freedom. By this I mean to say, evil is a privileged occasion for becoming aware of freedom. What does it actually mean to impute my own acts to myself? It is, first of all, to assume the consequences of these acts for the future; that is, he who has acted is also he who will admit the fault, who will repair the damage, who will bear the blame. In other words, I offer myself as the bearer of the sanction. I agree to enter into the dialectic of praise and blame. But in placing myself before the consequences of my act, I refer myself back to the moment prior to my act, and I designate my-self as he who not only performed the act, but who could have done otherwise. This conviction of having done something freely is not a matter of observation. It is once again a performative: I declare myself, after the fact, as being he who could have done otherwise; this "after the fact" is the backlash of taking upon oneself the consequences. He who takes the consequences upon himself declares himself free, and discerns this freedom as already at work in the incriminated act. At that point I can say that I have committed the act. This movement from in front of to behind the responsibility is essential. It constitutes the identity of the moral subject through past, present and future. He who *will* bear the blame is the same who *now* takes the act upon him-self and he who *has* acted. I posit the identity of him who accepts the future responsibilities of his act, and he who has acted. And the two dimensions, future and past, are linked in the present. The future of sanction and the past of action committed are tied together in the present of confession.

Such is the first stage of reflection in the experience of evil:

the reciprocal constitution of the signification of *free* and the signification of *evil* is a specific performative: *confession*. The second moment of reflection concerns the link between evil and obligation. I do not at all want to discuss the meaning of expressions such as "You ought" nor their relation with the predicates "Good" and "Evil". This problem is well known to English philosophy. My contribution to a reflection on evil will be limited to this problem: let us take as our point of departure, the expression and the experience "I could have done otherwise". This is, as we have seen, an implication of the act by which I impute to myself the responsibility for a past act. But the awareness that one could have done otherwise is closely linked to the awareness that one *should* have done otherwise. It is because I recognize my "ought" that I recognize my "could". A being who is obligated is a being who presumes that he can do what he should do. We are well aware of the usage to which Kant put this affirmation: you must, therefore you can. It is certainly not an argument, in the sense that I could deduce the possibility from the obligation. I would rather say that the "ought" serves here as a detector: if I feel, or believe, or know that I am obligated, it is because I am a being that can act, not only under the impulsion or constraint of desire and fear, but under the condition of a law which I represent to myself. In this sense Kant is right: to act according to the representation of a law is something other than to act according to laws. This power of acting according to the representation of a law is the will. But this discovery has long-range consequences: for in discovering the power to follow the law (or that which I consider as the law for myself) I discover also the *terrible* power of acting *against*. (Indeed, the experience of remorse which is the experience of the relation between freedom and obligation is a twofold experience: on the one hand, I recognize an obligation, and therefore a power corresponding to this obligation, but I admit to having acted against the law which continues to appear to me as obligatory. This is commonly called a transgression.) Freedom is the power to act according to the representation of a law *and* not to meet the obligation. ("Here is what I should have done, therefore what I could have done, and look at what I did." The imputation of the past act is thus morally qualified by its relation to the "ought" and "can".) By the same fact, a new determination of evil and a new determination of freedom appear together, in addition to the forms of reciprocity which are described above. The new determination of evil can be expressed in Kantian terms: it is the reversal of the relation between motive and law, interior to the maxim of my action. This definition is to be understood as follows: if I call a maxim the practical enunciation of what I propose to do, evil is nothing in itself; it has neither physical nor psychical reality; it is only an inverted relationship; it is a relation, not a thing, a relation inverted with regard to the order of preference and subordination indicated by obligation. In this way, we have achieved a "de-realization" of evil: not only does evil exist only in the act of taking it upon oneself, of assuming it, of claiming it, but what characterizes it, from a moral point of view, is the order in which an agent disposes of his maxims; it is a preference which ought not to have been (an inverted relation within the maxim of action).

But a new determination of freedom appears at the same time. I spoke a moment ago of the *terrible* power of acting against. It is, indeed, in the confession of evil that I discover the power of subversion of the will. Let us call it the *arbitrary*, to translate the German *Willkur*, which is at the same time free choice, i.e., the power of contraries, that which we recognized in the consciousness that one could have done otherwise, and in the power not to follow an obligation which I simultaneously recognize as just.

Have we exhausted the meaning of evil for ethics? I do not think so. In the "Essay on Radical Evil" which begins *Religion within the Limits of Reason Alone*, Kant poses the problem of a common origin of all evil maxims; indeed, we have not gone far in a reflection on evil, as long as we consider separately one bad intention, and then another, and again another. "We must conclude," says Kant, "from many, or even from a single conscious evil action, *a priori* to an evil maxim as its foundation, and from this maxim to a general foundation inherent in the subject, of all morally bad maxims, a foundation which in its own turn would be a maxim, so that finally we could qualify a man as evil" (38-9).

This movement towards greater depth which goes from evil maxims to their evil foundation is the philosophical transposition of the movement of sins to sin (in the singular) of which we spoke in Part I, on the level of symbolic expressions, and in particular of myth. Among other things, the myth of Adam signifies that all sins are referred to a unique root, which is, in some way or other, anterior to each of the particular expressions of evil, yet the myth could be told because the confessing community raised itself to the level of a confession of evil as involving all men. It is because the community confesses a fundamental guilt that the myth can describe the unique coming to be of evil as an event which happens only once. The Kantian doctrine of radical evil is an attempt to recapture philosophically the experience of this myth.

What qualifies this re-examination as philosophical? Essentially the treatment of radical evil as the foundation of multiple evil maxims. It is therefore upon this notion of foundation that we should bring our critical effort to bear.

Now, what do we mean by a foundation of evil maxims? We might well call it an *a priori* condition in order to emphasize that it is not a fact to be observed or a temporal origin to be retraced. It is not an empirical fact, but a first disposition of freedom that must be supposed so that the universal spectacle of human evil can be offered to experience. Neither is it a temporal origin, for this theory would lead back to a natural causality. Evil would cease to be evil, if it ceased to be "a manner of being of freedom, which itself comes from freedom". Therefore, evil does not have an origin in the sense of an antecedent cause. "Every evil action, when pushed back to its rational origin, should be considered as if man had arrived at it directly from the state of innocence" (62). (Everything is in this "as if". It is the philosophical equivalent of the myth of the fall; it is the rational myth of the coming-to-be of evil, of the instantaneous passage from innocence to sin; as Adam [rather than *in* Adam] we originate evil.)

But what is this unique coming-to-be which contains within itself all evil maxims? It must be admitted that we have no further concept for thinking of an evil will.

For this coming-to-be is not at all an act of my arbitrary will, which I could do or not do. For the enigma of this foundation is that reflection discovers, as a fact, that freedom has already chosen in an evil way. This evil is already there. It is in this sense that it is radical, that is, anterior, as a non-temporal aspect of every evil intention, of every evil action.

But this failure of reflection is not in vain; it succeeds in giving a character, proper to a *philosophy of limit*, and in distinguishing itself from a philosophy of system, such as that of Hegel.

The limit is twofold: limit of my knowledge, limit of my power. On the one hand, *I do not know* the origin of my evil liberty; this non-knowledge of the origin is essential to the very act of confession of my radically evil freedom. The non-knowledge is a part of the performative of confession, or, in other words, of my self-recognition and self-appropriation. On the other hand, I discover the *non-power* of my freedom. (Curious non-power, for I declare that I am responsible for this non-power. This non-power is completely different from the claim of an outside constraint.) I claim that my freedom has already made itself not-free. This admission is the greatest paradox of ethics. It seems to contradict our point of departure. We began by saying: evil is what I could have not done; this remains true. But at the same time I claim: evil is this prior captivity, which makes it so that I must do evil. This contradiction is interior to my freedom, it marks the non-power of power, the non-freedom of freedom.

Is this a lesson in despair? Not at all: this admission is, on the contrary, the access to a point where everything can begin again. The return to the origin is a return to that place where freedom discovers itself, as something to be delivered—in brief, to that place where it can *hope* to be delivered.

III. Religious Dimension

I have just attempted with the aid of the philosophy of Kant to characterize the problem of evil as an ethical problem. It is the twofold relation of evil to obligation and to freedom, which has seemed to me to characterize the problem of evil as an ethical problem.

Now, if I ask what is the specifically religious way of speaking about evil, I would not hesitate for a moment to answer: the language is that of hope. This thesis requires an explanation. Leaving aside for a moment the question of evil, to which I shall return later, I would like to justify the central role of hope in Christian theology. Hope has rarely been the central concept in theology. And yet, we now know, since the work of Johannes

Weiss and Albert Schweitzer, that the preaching of Jesus was concerned essentially with the Kingdom of God: the Kingdom is at hand; the Kingdom has drawn near to us; the Kingdom is in your midst. If the preaching of Jesus and of the primitive Church thus proceeds from an eschatological perspective, we should re-think all of theology from this eschatological viewpoint. But this revision of theological concepts, taking its point of departure from the exegesis of the New Testament, centred on the preaching of the Kingdom-to-come, finds support in a parallel revision of the theology of the Old Testament. Thus Martin Buber contrasts the God of the promise—God of the desert and of the wandering—with the popular gods who manifest themselves in natural epiphanies, in the figure of the king or in the idols of the temple. The God who comes is a *name*, the god who shows himself is an *idol*. The God of the promise opens up a history, the god of epiphanies animates a nature. But the New Testament did not put an end to the theology of the Promise, for the Resurrection itself, which is at the centre of its message, is not only the fulfilment of the promise in a unique event, but the confirmation of the promise which becomes for all the hope of final victory over death.

What follows from this for freedom and for evil, which ethical consciousness has grasped in their unity? I shall begin by a discussion of freedom, for a reason which will become clear in a moment. It seems to me that religion is distinguished from ethics in the fact that it requires that we think of freedom under the sign of hope.

In the language of the Gospel, I would say: to consider freedom in the light of hope is to re-situate my existence in the movement, which might be called, with Jürgen Moltmann, the "future of the resurrection of Christ". This "kerygmatic" formula can be translated in several ways in contemporary language. First of all, with Kierkegaard, we could call freedom in the light of hope the "passion for the *possible*"; this formula, in contrast to all wisdom of the present, to all submission to necessity, underscores the imprint of the promise on freedom. Freedom, entrusted to the "God who comes", is open to the radically new; it is the creative imagination of the possible.

But, in a deeper dimension, freedom *in the light of* hope is a freedom which affirms itself, *in spite of* death, and in spite of all the signs of death; for, in a phrase of the Reformers, the Kingdom is hidden *sub contrario*, under its contrary, the cross. Freedom in the light of hope is freedom for the denial of death, freedom to decipher the signs of the Resurrection under the contrary appearance of death.

Likewise, the category of "in spite of..." is the opposite or reverse side of a vital thrust, of a perspective of belief which finds its expression in the famous "how much more" of St. Paul. This category, more fundamental than the "in spite of", expresses what might be called the logic of the superabundance, which is the logic of hope. Here the words of St Paul to the Romans come to mind: "But the free gift is not like the fault, for, if many died through one man's fault, *how much more* have the grace of God and the gift conferred by the grace of that one man, Jesus Christ, abounded for many.... If because of one man's fault, death reigned through that one man, *how much more* will those who receive the abundance of grace, the free gift of righteousness, reign in life through the one man Jesus Christ.... Law came in to increase the fault; but where sin increased, grace abounded all the more..." (Rom. 5. 15, 17, 20).

This logic of surplus and excess is to be uncovered in daily life, in work and in leisure, in politics and in universal history. The "in spite of" which keeps us in readiness for the denial is only the inverse, the shadow side, of this joyous "how much more" by which freedom feels itself, knows itself and wills itself to belong to this economy of superabundance.

This notion of an economy of superabundance permits us to return to the problem of evil. It is from this point of departure, and in it, that a religious or theological discourse on evil can be held. Ethics has said all it can about evil in calling it: (1) a work of freedom; (2) a subversion of the relation of the maxim to the law; (3) an unfathomable disposition of freedom which makes it unavailable to itself.

Religion uses another language about evil. And this language keeps itself entirely within the limits of the perimeter of the promise and under the sign of hope. First of all, this language places evil *before* God. "Against you, against you alone have I sinned, I have done evil in your sight." This invocation which transforms the moral confession into a confession of sin, appears, at first glance, to be an intensification in the consciousness of evil. But that is an illusion, the moralizing illusion of Christianity. Situated before God, evil is installed again in the movement of the promise: the invocation is already the beginning of the restoration of a bond, the initiation of a new creation. The "passion for the possible" has already taken possession of the confession of evil; repentance, essentially directed towards the future, has already cut itself off from remorse which is a brooding reflection on the past.

Next, religious language profoundly changes the very content of the consciousness of evil. Evil in moral consciousness is essentially transgression, that is, subversion of the law; it is in this way that the majority of pious men continue to consider sin. And yet, situated before God, evil is qualitatively changed; it consists less in a transgression of a law than in a pretension of man to be master of his life. The will to live according to the law is, therefore, also an expression of evil—and even the most deadly, because the most dissimulated: worse than injustice is one's own justice. Ethical consciousness does not know this, but religious consciousness does. But this second discovery can also be expressed in terms of promise and hope.

Indeed, the will is not constituted, as we have seemed to believe in the context of the ethical analysis, merely by the relation between the arbitrary and the law (in Kantian terms, between the *Willkür* or arbitrary will and the *Wille* or determination by the law of reason). The will is more fundamentally constituted by a desire of fulfilment or achievement. Kant himself, in the dialectical part of the *Critique of Practical Reason*, recognized this intended goal of totalization. It is this precisely which animates the *Dialectic of Practical Reason*, as the relation to the law animates the *Analytic*. Now this tendency towards totalization, according to Kant, requires the reconciliation of two moments which Rigorism has separated: "Virtue", that is, obedience to pure duty, and happiness, that is, satisfaction of desire. This reconciliation is the Kantian equivalent of hope. This rebound of the philosophy of will entails a rebound of the philosophy of evil. If the tendency towards totalization is thus the soul of the

will, we have not yet reached the foundation of the problem of
evil so long as we have kept it within the limits of a reflection of
the relations of the arbitrary and the law. The true evil, the evil
of evil, shows itself in false syntheses, i.e., in contemporary falsi-
fications of the great undertakings of totalization of cultural experience, that is, in political and ecclesiastical institutions. In
this way, evil shows its true face—the evil of evil is the lie of
premature syntheses, of violent totalizations.

Evil "abounds" wherever man transcends himself in grandiose
undertakings, wherein he sees the culmination of his existence
in the higher works of culture, in politics and in religion. And
so, these great simulacra, the cult of race, the cult of the State
and all forms of false worship, are the very birth of idols, sub-
stituted for the "Name", who should remain faceless.

But this greater deepening of our understanding of evil is, once
again, a conquest of hope: it is because man is a goal of totality
a will of total fulfilment, that he plunges himself into totali-
tarianisms, which really constitute the pathology of hope. As the
old proverb says, demons haunt only the courts of the gods. But,
at the same time, we sense that evil itself is a part of the economy
of superabundance. Paraphrasing St Paul, I dare to say: Wherever
evil "abounds", hope "super-abounds". We must therefore have
the courage to incorporate evil into the epic of hope. In a way that
we know not, evil itself co-operates, works towards the advance-
ment of the Kingdom of God. This is the viewpoint of faith on
evil. This view is not that of the moralist; the moralist contrasts
the *predicate* evil with the predicate good; he condemns evil; he
imputes it to freedom; and finally, he stops at the limit of the inscrutable; for we do not know how it is possible that freedom
could be enslaved. Faith does not look in this direction; the
origin of evil is not its problem; the end of evil is its problem.
With the prophets, faith incorporates this end into the economy
of the promise, with Jesus, into the preaching of the God who
comes, with St Paul, into the law of superabundance. This is
why the view of faith on events and on men is essentially bene-
volent. Faith justifies the man of the *Aufklärung* for whom, in
the great romance of culture, evil is a factor in the education of
the human race, rather than the puritan, who never succeeds in
taking the step from condemnation to mercy, and who thus

remains within the ethical dimension, and never enters into the perspective of the Kingdom which comes.

Such are the three "discourses" which may be held about guilt: the *semantic* discourse is mainly a phenomenology of confession by means of an interpretation of symbolic expressions; the *ethical* discourse is an explanation of the relation between freedom, obligation and evil (it relies on the performatives through which I take on myself the origin of evil and constitute myself as a responsible will); the *religious* discourse is a reinterpretation of freedom and evil in the light of hope—in Christian terms, of hope in the universal resurrection from the dead.

If I consider these three discourses as a whole, they offer a kind of progression, which could be compared to the progression from the aesthetic stage to the ethical and the religious stage in Kierkegaard's philosophy. I should accept this comparison, if I did not find it disparaging and discouraging.*

* This article has already appeared in *Le conflit des herméneutics* (Paris, Editions du Seuil), a collection of articles by Paul Ricoeur.

Wolf-Dieter Marsch

Is Consciousness of Sin "False Consciousness"?

FOR some three thousand years Jewish-Christian tradition has recognized men not as "justified" but as "guilty" before their God. This recognition has implied that no individual can efface his "sinfulness" by virtue of intelligence, goodwill or pious works, and that from the beginning mankind has been held in an uninterrupted context of collective guilt that no human impulse could abrogate (*peccatum originale, vitium originis*). For some three hundred years the West European Enlightenment tradition has acknowledged a "false consciousness", arising in the circumstances of social life and brought about by political suasions, by the conditions peculiar to civil society and by class distinctions and social attitudes. This "false consciousness" has been seen as so obstructing, distorting and rendering impossible a truly human social life that it cannot be removed merely by adopting a "correct consciousness" (Francis Bacon: the *idola theatri* and *idola fori*); nevertheless, the hope persists that a transformation of political and social conditions will at the same time affect the growth of consciousness, whether by education, enlightenment or force.

What is the connection between these two convictions? They are neither identical nor wholly disparate. Sin in the sight of God is something other than the growth of prejudice and the formation of an ideology. Atonement, salvation and the forgiveness of sins are not synonymous with a "true", humanly enlightened consciousness. But there is a connection in so far as both denote an historically existential and collective relationship—a "destructive structure"[1]—that is conceived as evil and in which the individual man is ensnared through no fault of his own, even though he is held responsible for it. In this article I shall try to assess the extent to which the two affirmations agree or differ. Before offering a final comparative analysis (II), I shall discuss the biblical understanding of sin and the history of the concept of ideology (I).

I. THE NOTIONS OF SIN AND IDEOLOGY

1. In Theology and Scripture

From the third century A.D. Western Christian tradition has interpreted the biblical "sin" and "original sin" as the forfeiture of godlike immortality and of an openness to good (*similitudo Dei*) that were originally proper to man, and as a tendency to covetousness (*concupiscentia*) passed on from parents to their children— a subjectivity that is unconsciously and consciously opposed to God's will. The sinful nature of this contradiction (*reatus*) can, as it were, be held in check by the bestowal of grace through the sacraments of the Church (in baptism and penance, and through justification). For the purposes of this system of pastoral and sacramental control, medieval and post-Tridentine Catholicism divided sin as sin into original, mortal, capital and venial sin. The Reformation shattered this systematization of sin by restoring a unique state of guilt to a position of central importance: "*sine metu Dei, sine fiducia erga Deum*"[2] is the condition of the sinful man who does not put himself in a position of total submission to God and receive his salvation through Christ.

In more modern times this radical desacramentalization of the concept of sin led increasingly to the characterization of sin as an inward and essentially private perversion of existence before God —a desperate desire for self-sufficiency and an inability to be free (Kierkegaard), wholly without involvement in the circumstances of social life. The Catholic doctrine of sin may well have

---

[1] Paul Tillich (in *Systematische Theologie*, vol. 2, Stuttgart, 1958) offers this description of the consequences of original sin and sees it as the "existential self-destruction" of mankind "alienated" from its original condition.

[2] *Confessio Augustana*, art. II, *Bek. schr. d. ev.-luth. Kirchen* (Göttingen, 1930), vol. 1, p. 52.

been faulted for excessive moralization and repressive casuistry, but the Protestant teaching was excessively individualized, and all the more so as the environment and society were experienced in increasingly "worldly" and secular terms: the cause of sinfulness could no longer be sought in materially (technologically) and politically ordained conditions but in the individual alone; the struggle between good and evil, sin and redemption, was carried on in the human heart and conscience.

The biblical, and primarily the Old Testament meaning of the term "sin" points in a quite different direction: it is not restricted semantically to any one referent. Sin can mean failure in one's responsibilities towards others, which implies at the same time guilt in the sight of God; it can also signify the evil distortion of a "perverted action", or even "rebelliousness"—which meant originally the contestation of legal estate. All three meanings primarily refer not to individual, private sentiments but to the connection between the deed that disturbs the divinely willed union of brotherhood, and the resulting punishment: "Man's action on the one hand and its consequence on the other ... are not yet understood as two separate and self-sufficient phenomena."[3] The action which destroys community and self, whether an offence against the cult, the law or the ethical code, and its consequence, which requires an expiatory restoration of sacral order, are not dissociated; the social and political destiny of man and man's sin, the destruction of the divine union, are interconnected.

But there is the problem of original sin, which Israel explicated by means of the aetiological image of the "Fall" (Gen. 3. 1–24) and its consequences as recounted by the Yahwist. The Garden of Eden is seen as an oasis in which grows the "tree of knowledge of good and evil", that is, the practical symbol of omnipotence, omniscience and boundlessness,[4] the fruit of which man, originally given dominion over every living creature and the ability to live in concord with his fellows, may not eat. Out of a mixture of desire for experimentation, feminine curiosity

[3] G. von Rad, *Theologie des Alten Testaments*, vol. 1 (Munich, 1957), pp. 264 and 261 ff.
[4] Cf. G. von Rad, *Das erste Buch Mose* (ATD 2-4) (Göttingen, 1953), pp. 65 f. and 70 f.

and thirst for knowledge, men overstep the bounds set them. This has been called the first act of existential self-manipulation —the beginning of a self-generated history that no longer respects any limit ordained for finite beings. This action "had irreversible consequences and inaugurated a process that humanity cannot abrogate by returning to the time before it started"—"a history that flows one way only and cannot be turned back".[5]

The results of this action, expressed in the sentence pronounced by Yahweh, are: estrangement between men (shame at nakedness, conflict between generations), alienation between man and his physical make-up (the anguish of death and birth, needless labour) and alienation of man from his natural environment (the enmity of the beasts, the unfruitfulness of the earth). Further consequences are: the destruction of co-operative endeavour through fratricide (Gen. 4. 1 ff.), the increasing division of labour (Gen. 4. 20 ff.), union with the sons of Elohim (Gen. 6. 1 ff.), drunkenness and shamelessness (Gen. 9. 20 ff.), titanic building and confusion of language (Gen. 11. 1 ff.). In this "one-way" self-produced historical existence, therefore, quite "normal" situations are represented as sins with the punishable consequences of sin. *In these situations God repeatedly displays his mercy*: he does not let mankind perish in the deluge (Gen. 6. 5–8, 22); he makes a new covenant with Noah which once again expressly confirms the dominion of man over his environment, and condemns only murder (Gen. 9. 1 ff.); with God's blessing on the exodus of Abraham, Israel advances into the light of history.

This representation of the *causa peccati* in the categories of myth implies that sin does not belong to the *physical constitution* of man (not even to the corruption of its sexual aspect) but to his *social and political destiny*. Through quite "normal" reactions and behaviour, such as curiosity, scepticism, the need for differentiation, aggression and the desire to demonstrate and dominate, mankind manipulates itself into "alienated" ways of life, while looking back to a primordial age of "dreamlike guiltlessness",[6]

[5] Cf. Karl Rahner, "Experiment Mensch. Theologisches über die Selbstmanipulation des Menschen", in *Die Frage nach dem Menschen. Festchrift für Max Müller* (Freiburg/Munich, 1966), p. 61. See also pp. 45 ff.

[6] Paul Tillich (*op. cit.*, pp. 39 ff.) interprets the symbol of the original state of man thus, in accordance with the tradition of German idealism.

and forward to an ultimate liberation from the burdens, destruction and guilt of a finite existence.

The transcendence of "dreamlike guiltlessness" and transcendence over and beyond apparently culpable historical conditions
belong together. When we today confirm that the now extremely
diffuse concept of "alienation" does have a rational core in the
maiming of the structure of social roles by forms of "behavioural
disturbance" that are actually painful and injurious to experience
and verge upon the pathological,[7] we may infer that the Old
Testament consciousness of sin can *also* be expressed as "false
consciousness". It contradicts a "true consciousness" to which
man is open as the creature of God. Only in contradicting what
ought not to be does man comprehend his very truth. Of course,
in the Bible the norms of measurement for the "true" or the
"false" in this case are not to be taken from social interaction,
but are ordained or "given" by God, who has *set* the limits for
man and made known to him (that is, made him "conscious" of)
his *mortality*. God alone knows and dictates what is good and
evil; in the sacred partnership of his covenant with man there is
God's "Law", which is designed to restrict the destructive tendencies of man. But these commandments, which controlled cult,
ethics and jurisdiction in Israel, have to be understood existen-
tially and historically, and must be constantly renewed: the will
of God and the fulfilment of social identity which man strives
after in his attempt to transcend, and ever and again culpably
falls short of, are closely related.[8] "True consciousness", which
is directed towards the will of God, reaches beyond the circumstances of finite mortal history, but is not dissociated from them.
Central notions of a fulfilled social identity such as "peace"
(*shalom*) or justice (*sedaqua*) are expressions of a political salvation that Israel manifestly never experienced.

This unfulfilled and therefore utopian and open covenant
eventually found a more emphatically personal expression, above
all in the prophetic pronouncements on sin: God's holy will and

[7] Cf. H. P. Dreitzel, *Die gesellschaftlichen Leiden und das Leiden an
der Gesellschaft* (Stuttgart, 1968), pp. 18 ff.

[8] In his theory of the creation (*Kirchliche Dogmatik*, vol. III/1–4), Karl
Barth also repeatedly emphasizes this connection between God's coven-
anted faith and social identity.

summons are opposed to the sinfully perverted heart of man; the more inscrutable God's transcendence and his punishments (sickness, war, banishment and loss of national identity), the more unfathomable the depths of the sinful subjectivity of man apart from God—until the quest for "holy conditions of life" wholly disappeared with Wisdom literature (Job) and in the Apocalyptic writings was separated into the dualism of a totally lost "old aeon" and a supernatural "new aeon" of the future.

Under the influence of this dualistic approach, in the New Testament (particularly in Paul and in John) sin is conceived of within limits that are to be interpreted more in cosmic and exis-tentialist than in social and political terms. Sin is taken to be a "trans-subjective force"[9] which wholly dominates "carnal" man and allows him to lapse into self-glorification and concupiscence. But with Christ, whose death and resurrection achieve the signi-ficance of a cosmic metamorphosis, a "spiritual" man is born who is free from sin and has put death and transience behind him. Such actualities as Adam's transgression disappear behind the typological confrontation between the "old" and the "new" man(kind) (Rom. 5. 6); and the law is formalized as judgment in comparison with the Old Testament: it is that sphere of power which effects sin and death in which post-Adamitic man lives (Rom. 7), and from which the action of Christ, as a demonstra-tion of the baseless loving-kindness of God, liberates mankind.

This dualism of sin and grace, of death and life, and of perdi-tion and salvation (which has of course encouraged a de-politiciza-tion of the understanding of sin in Christian theology), is only partly grounded on the preaching and activity of Jesus. Un-doubtedly there is a "political" dimension to his preaching of the kingdom of God in the promise of the presence of God pre-cisely to the "publicans and sinners" (Matt. 11. 9)—those despair-ing of religion, the sick, the unclassed and the despised; a God who makes "his sun to rise on the evil and on the good" (Matt. 5. 45). Not the fulfilment of a cultic or ethical commandment, and not the keeping of the prescriptions of a fixed divine ordi-nance, decides whether a man is "sinful" or "just", but human and direct faith in Jesus and the personal authority embodied in

[9] R. Conzelmann, *Grundriss der Theologie des Neuen Testaments* (Munich, 1967), p. 217.

him, behind which stands the infinitely demanding and infinitely giving Lord. A sentence such as "Thy sins be forgiven thee"
(Mk. 2. 5 par.) is virtually identical with "Thy faith hath made
thee whole" (Mk. 10. 52 par.). Sin can consist only in *not* following this direct humanly co-operative claim, not wishing to recognize the nearness of God and the removal of "alienation" with
Jesus, and withdrawal from the "new life" which "overcomes
alienation under the conditions of alienated existence".[10] This
new life, the conviction of the sovereignty of God, is openly manifest only in the word of exhortation and consolation, in significant actions and in the utopian hope that the humanity of Jesus
which perished on the cross belongs to the future. "True consciousness" in Jesus' sense would consist in hoping for the realization of the presence of God in Jesus, without surrendering the
actuality and limitation of finite existence.

2. *Philosophically and Politically*

The notion of "false consciousness" that has prevailed since the
Enlightenment presupposes that man, by means of experience and
reason, can acquire a "true consciousness" and apply it politically. For him there are no longer any truths above history or
limiting ordinances; social existence, the circumstances of society
and the conditions of domination, must contain the causes of
man's adoption of a "false consciousness" (ideologies, prejudices,
illusions in regard to his actual situation, theoretical justifications
of examples of concrete destitution) and his falling short of a
humane goal in social life (freedom, justice, equality, brotherli-
ness). Such men live "non-contemporaneously",[11] that is, not in
a way corresponding to the human possibilities of their own time,
but still ensnared in the surviving fragments of past structures.
    One might divide the consideration of the possibility of

[10] Paul Tillich (*op. cit.*, pp. 107 ff.) describes Jesus' appearance as that
of the "beginning and power" of an alienated existence which has been
overcome in principle.
[11] Ernst Bloch has used the terms "non-contemporaneity" and "non-
contemporaneous contradiction" to characterize before all else the "German ideology" of the Twenties, in *Erbschaft dieser Zeit* (Frankfurt, 1962),
pp. 111 ff., 45 ff.

ideology in modern political philosophy into three stages:[12] In the first stage (which can be said to extend from Francis Bacon and David Hume to the French Encyclopaedists and then to Ludwig Feuerbach) there is a basic, comparatively naïve trust in the openness to enlightenment of human reason, which deems it capable of seeing through the socially conditioned illusions as such—those *"idola"* or "graven images" in whose perpetuation monarchs, priests and economically dominant concerns have a massive interest. The "false consciousness", which holds fast to religious hopes in a world beyond, to metaphysical ideas and to theoretical justifications of outdated social structures, can be exposed as a deception of practical reason. This a-historical faith in enlightened and emancipated reason was soon disqualified as being itself "ideological" (Napoleon's conflict with the "ideologues"). But the historical philosophy of German idealism (Hegel) was the first to offer a differentiated apparatus for more precise analysis of the interplay of reason and interest, of human emancipation and politically influenced alienation.

In particular, historical and dialectical materialism (Karl Marx) inaugurated a second stage in the analysis of "false consciousness". Marx criticized both the naïve materialism which imagined that all "spiritual" images and values could be traced to political and economic causes, and the hope of his friends, the Young Hegelians, in a purely "human" emancipation from the uncomprehended forces of domination—when that hope was not accompanied by political and revolutionary action (*praxis*). The real antagonisms of history (class struggles, the opposition between the exploiters and the exploited, and the rise of new social classes towards power and riches) are the basis for the growth of a "true consciousness", that is, in the conflict of interests. Social practice defines what is true and false; the search for ideological justifications (which once more ordain an alienated *praxis*) is a secondary consideration. In any case, the theoretical critique of "false consciousness" and the practical and political will to bring about actual changes must work hand in hand, or else there can be no hope that a "true consciousness" will emerge.

Of course a necessary presupposition of this solution of the

[12] Cf. K. Lenk (ed.), *Ideologie, Ideologiekritik und Wissenssoziologie* (Soziologische Texte, vol. 4, Neuwied, 1961).

problem of ideology is that man, as a properly collective being capable of social organization, can see himself as the sole creative subject of history: "as far as socialist man is concerned . . . the whole of so-called world history is no more than . . . the production of man through human work, no more than the development of nature for man".[13] To assume a transcendence of history as a whole—divine precepts and promises for the future, or even a mere *telos* of salvation history that, in utopian style, precedes its realization—is, as far as Marx is concerned, just as senseless as any thought of the world and man as created, and therefore as any musing on limits to finite existence.[14] For man who creates himself the only limits are the economic and political conditions which necessarily result in a "false consciousness", and which can be removed only by revolutionary action. In order to be rid of them one requires a group of men who are practically (as the class of the industrially exploited) and theoretically (as the radically self-alienated) in a position to realize a "true consciousness": the proletariat.

A century of social history has shown that this mediator of salvation in the form of an all-creative subject of revolutionary emancipation simply does not exist. Socialist systems have come to power with the aid of *élites* of Party cadres who have had to use suffering and force in order to inculcate a "true consciousness" in the masses. Therefore the quest for the origins of "false consciousness" underwent a significant change in social philosophy after Marx (one might call it a third stage of research into the nature of ideology). The question was asked whether all social existence was not basically pre- and a-logically conditioned by affects, drives, unconscious motivations and irrational reactions which could be theoretically vindicated only secondarily. Such "residues" (Pareto), which are at the basis of social dynamics, are of course no longer accessible to the search for a "true consciousness". Only the deduced "derivations" of social behaviour are rationally analysable. Or: Does not civilization—life in common according to the achievement principle, political domination and

[13] Karl Marx, *Werke*, ed. J. Lieber (Darmstadt, 1962), pp. 568, 607.
[14] Cf. *op. cit., supra*, where Marx opposes the theory of a creation of the world and man, which is for him an "illusionary abstraction from natural and human existence".

conventional structures of order—force man to the conscious denial or repression of the drives and demands of the libido, so that the man repressed by civilization becomes really aware of the problem of a "false consciousness" only when he can allow his latent libido to "live" and to realize a "new sensibility" in relation to the principles of pleasure and achievement (Sigmund Freud, Herbert Marcuse)? Or: Aren't all ideas of a "true consciousness"—whether as God's plan for salvation or as images of human emancipation and a successful identity of man and his world—explicable only as "vacuous formulas" or anthropomorphic (and sociomorphic or technomorphic) projections, which man forges for himself in order to provide the meaningless process of history with a subsequent meaning (Nietzsche, F. Topitsch)? Then the analysis of "false consciousness" can be limited to the local demonstration of the socially conditioned character of all knowledge—the "attachment of knowledge to existence" (Karl Mannheim); or to the critical representation to man, lost in the "delusive nexus" of society, of the extent of his delusion (Theodor Adorno).

In any case, philosophy after Marx, in so far as it is not itself ideological, must avoid taking an historical subject as a subject of liberation from "false consciousness", and supposing categories such as "true" and "false" to be applicable to social processes. In order to avoid the stultification of positivistic confirmation of what happens "anyhow", or of technocratic regulation, a philosophy which claims to hold fast to the Enlightenment tradition of the search for emancipation must limit itself to the "check on achievement" method (Jürgen Habermas): by this, a society is confronted critically with what it claims to be, and then the "interest" of reason is traced—critically—in the actual and material processes of society. Reason which considers itself duty-bound to the "truth" of emancipatory enlightenment can do no more than this.

II. ANALOGIES AND DIFFERENCES

It should already have become clear how far the Jewish-Christian consciousness of sin and the philosophical-sociological analysis of false consciousness are analogous, and to what extent they differ. To summarize:

1. *The Historicity of Salvation*

Those "destructive structures" which oppose the human determination of man are to be found in human society and not in
man's nature as such. Interpretation of the traditional biblical
history of evil has always to be directed to quite normal inclinations and events of historical transcendence such as inquisitive-
ness, scepticism, self-sufficiency, the generation of a "false consciousness"—inclinations and events which result in men—as
once in the garden of Eden—having to consider their life as alienated and devoid of salvation. Their history does not appear to
them as a process of degeneracy and misfortune, *beyond* which
their only destiny is salvation; instead the question of and quest
for a "true consciousness" that could overcome the phenomena
of alienation arises *in* the historical conflicts and contradictions
between what is humanly possible and humanly actual. The
modern problem of ideology, the analysis of "false consciousness", is—initially, at any rate—similar to the Old Testament understanding of sin. There are quite rationally tractable grounds
for the suffering of socialized humanity under what humanity
itself has created in the economic and political structures of labour
and domination. Humankind can and must be confronted critically with its own claims and aims. Material conditions and
theories which are "guilty"—responsible for the fate of alienation
—can and must be discerned. Guilt is not simply a question
of individual morality but a collective political problem; it
resides in the contradictions between what is desired and intended, and what actually happens; contradictions in which men
clearly involve themselves in the course of the process of socialization, technologization and domination. So long as something like
unalienated human existence, free of the ideological confusions of
a "false consciousness", is conceivable, the quest for the causes
of the difference between origin and determination will persist.
Man is capable of salvation, and evil has historical and political
grounds.

Of course there is an irremovable difference between the
Jewish-Christian conception of sin, and ideology conceived of as
"false consciousness". The Jewish-Christian tradition recognizes
sin committed "before God", that is, in conscious knowledge of

bounds set for mankind (the tree of knowledge of good and evil), of an established and recommended community (the broken covenant), of a human possibility which is known and realized by men as not their own (Christ as the salvific event that changes the course of history), and of a human future that no man can forge for himself (the kingdom of God as utopia). Neither the mere enlightenment of a "false consciousness" nor class warfare nor the revelation of drives and motivations can remove the guilty relationship, but only God who forgives, brings "new life", and freely liberates man from himself and from the history of the past. The event which is Jesus' humanity, which changes the course of history (which means his historic destiny, together with the effects wrought in and through the faithful), cannot be explained away as a mere campaign for enlightenment. The historical manifestations of salvation and evil must be referred to their transcendental substantiation. Guilt has to be forgiven, and existence must be renewed.

2. The Category of Totality

The critique of ideology and consciousness of sin meet in the search for a "totality" of history or of the social process. This quest is meaningless for a reason which limits itself "technically" to optimum functioning and to the adaptation of the individual to existing social systems—to goal-oriented, functional "know-how". But it is inevitable in all stages of the history of the concept of ideology for a reason that claims to distinguish "false" from "true" consciousness. Its interest[15] in the realization of what is truly and humanly reasonable cannot be achieved in specific end-means relations, but seizes on universal relations. For in order to disclose false consciousness as such, it is necessary to have (at least an ideal-utopian) idea of what could be "true": non-alienated humanity, the fulfilment of emancipation, the successful identity of reason and nature, the fulfilment of freedom and justice, and so on. Without even a postulatory pre-concept of a goal of the totality of history, the critical analysis of ideology would lose all

[15] See especially Jürgen Habermas, *Erkenntis und Interesse* (Frankfurt, 1968), pp. 234 ff., on the transcendental, historical and philosophical basis of a concern for reason.

meaning; "true consciousness" cannot be identical with positivistic and technical affinities and with adaptation to a social process that is in principle unanalysable. It is no matter of chance that the questioning of ideologies and their analysis began in an age when the realization was dawning that man himself was the reasoning and responsible subject of history who, through reason and in action, could generate the aim of history. It is just as little a matter of chance that the problem of ideology was just as diffuse and insoluble when it became apparent that this kind of almighty and self-generating subject of history could not be discerned, and that the goal of the totality of history was enclosed in the pluralistic mists of value judgments and world-views.

The Jewish-Christian experience of sin is also a matter of the "whole" of history; and the standards for a good life (justice, peace, co-operation) were necessarily general in nature—like the recognition of the evil in which men found themselves: Israel did not correspond to God's "covenant", and did not show itself to be his own people. And the more intensively Israel became interwoven with the history of the Near East, the more universal became the consideration of a "whole" in the face of which sin and guilt were clear: from the union of the twelve nomadic tribes to the world history at whose beginning and end stands the God who judges and saves. In the New Testament the destiny of an individual man is seen as the start of a wholly new aeon: in the resurrected and coming Christ everything is "made new"; the "kingdom of God" can be none other than a universal kingdom for all men; sin is characteristic of the totality of the world of death that is passing away.

Consideration of a "totality" of historical existence is an inescapable part of Jewish-Christian belief in God,[16] and also of the experience of sinning in the sight of God. The idea of a goal-oriented "world-history" was only possible as a concept in the first place on the basis of Christian theology, which removed divinity from the mundane but simultaneously subordinated the world to the dominion of God as the unity of a universal whole.

---

[16] Especially W. Pannenberg has systematized the connection between God and the totality of history. See *Grundfragen systematischer Theologie.* (Göttingen, 1967); *Theologie als Geschichte* (vol. 4 of *Neuland in der Theologie*, Zürich/Stuttgart, 1967).

Modern atheism is essentially founded upon the fact that this kind of "totality" of a divinely influenced universal history became increasingly imperceptible. The totality of historical existence and recognition of sin as "false consciousness" hang together.

But there is still an ineluctable difference between the consciousness of sin and a consideration of "false consciousness". The critique of ideology is inclined to press what it sees as the "true totality" on the individual ensnared in "false consciousness", whether by force, propaganda, education or denunciation. The truth can be made to count only in an antagonistic fashion, to the cost of the individuals who do not want to or cannot integrate themselves into this "totality". This tendency to oppress the individual is not inherent in the Christian consciousness of sin. For the God of the "whole" is simultaneously the wholly "personal" God who recognizes the individual before all else, forgives sins, and makes new beginnings possible in the particular even when the "whole" of history has not yet reached its goal. The category of reconciliation and expiation cannot be equated with integration into a "true whole" (Hegel). Sin in the face of the God of history remains the personal guilt of the free individual, which can only be forgiven the free individual.[17]

3. The Category of the "New"

Not only in the thought of Ernst Bloch but in all Enlightenment analysis of ideology the quest for radically "new life" is important. "False consciousness" must be overtaken as "old" and outdated. The consciousness of the nature of historical crises—the obsolescence of traditions and institutions and the negation of the past—is always inherent in the kind of critical thought that would treat history historically by taking it as malleable and open to change. From such a viewpoint the past becomes the mere prehistory of a new life that is signalled in the crises of the present moment. This new age is looked forward to as the ultimate, "eschatological" combination of theory and practice, the "community of the saved" and the final realization of humanity. Admittedly the ways and means of arriving at this new life differ.

[17] In "Die Frage nach Gott" (in *Grundfragen* ..., p. 361) Pannenberg has noted this irremovable interpenetration of universal totality and personal freedom in the Christian experience of God.

Is it to be achieved through the application of the intellect, through enlightenment and emancipation of the masses, through total revolutionary struggle, or by means of the restructuring of emotional needs? Is it also simultaneously and fatefully ordained by the antagonisms and latent tendencies of the present? Does it require an élitist party to put it into action? Whatever the answer may be, no one who criticizes or opposes "false consciousness" in the process of history can avoid seeing his own times as an epochal confrontation between the "old" and the "new". In so doing he sees "true consciousness" as something "temporal"— something that must occur in history and in time. The true is that which is new; history is experienced not as anamnesis—the return of and to the same—but as the process by which something that has never yet been is realized.

The Jewish-Christian understanding of sin also recognizes this basic temporality of God's truth. His good and his salvation are the future—the expected age of redemption which he promises will be fashioned out of the crises of the present. Israel experienced its history as a sequence of critical breaks with tradition. The sins of disruption of the covenant, disobedience and moral inadequacy were always followed by God's offering the chance of a new exodus—the entry into a land that he would show them. The salvific future of God is the new that never was, and which God now reveals. The past is seen in such a way that the judgments of the Lord are the "pre-history" of a possible humanization of man. The expiation of sins that have been committed (*teshuba, metanoia*, conversion) is always a process in time that separates the past "epochally" from that which is to come. There is continuity of history only in God, who forgives sin and makes totally new beginnings possible. In the New Testament, the assurance of forgiveness is synonymous with attainment to a future that fallen and sinful men cannot of themselves take for granted. In primitive Christian proclamation, Jesus' "Thy sins be forgiven thee" becomes the certainty that in Christ everything is made new.

But this new life is realized under the conditions of the old. Here ideology-critical and Christian thought are essentially different. Israel's hope in a new existence before God and a sanctified future implied no cancellation of history as already experienced, but rather constant reference to past evidence of the history of salvation: the covenant, the promised land, the stories of the patriarchs and the creation. And hope in Christ as the guarantor of a new humanity, as the Resurrected Christ, had always to be understood in connection with Jesus, the Crucified. Enthusiasm of and for history fulfilled always implied the non-fulfilment of the passion and solidarity with uncompensated suffering.[18] The new is never considered apart from the influences of the past, and Christian eschatology cannot be realized as the executed outline of a *dénouement* of humanity which is "true" because justified before God, but only as *eschatologia crucis*:[19] that is, as an outline of the future which, by faith in and knowledge of the destiny of Jesus, hopes for that which is new in the future of God.[20]

The consciousness of sin and "false consciousness" are certainly not identical. A Christian theology that would wholly identify guilt in the sight of God with the criticism of ideology, and make expiation or redemption synonymous with development aid, is undoubtedly in error. There is no evidence in the Bible of the concept of a fulfilment of man that can be generated by man himself. Instead, the phenomenon of sin forces man to have recourse to eternity, the irremovable difference between God and man. The consciousness of this distinction could make contemporary man (in so far as he is directed to the production of his history and the disclosure of the conflicts in this production) aware that "false consciousness" is removable not through corrective measures or by force, and that history cannot be fulfilled by man alone. So long as there is any consideration of the problem

---

[18] J. Moltmann has repeatedly referred to this tension in primitive Christian and particularly Pauline ethics. See especially "Die Kategorie Novum in der christlichen Theologie", in *Ernst Bloch zu ehren* (Frankfurt, 1965), pp. 244 ff., 249 ff., 256 ff.

[19] This concept has been used by Moltmann (*Theologie der Hoffnung*, Munich, 1964, p. 145; Eng. trans. *Theology of Hope*, London, 1968) in an attempt to reconcile the much-discussed contradiction between an eschatology of the future and one of the present in the New Testament.

[20] See for more detailed evidence: Wolf-Dieter Marsch, *Zukunft* (*Themen der Theologie*, vol. 2, Munich, 1969), pp. 142 ff.

of guilt in the sight of God and of its cancellation, conversion to a "true consciousness" is not in the hands of fallible and finite men.

Translated by John Griffiths

Louis Beirnaert

Psychoanalytical Theory and Moral Evil

WHEN psychoanalysis is made to throw light on ethics and vice versa, several difficulties emerge. Which kind of psychoanalysis is one talking about? Not only are different theories and practices grouped under this one heading, but the common image of psychoanalysis, linked to its inevitable appropriation by different ideologies and disciplines, also adds its quota of error to the way in which the problem is posed. Is one really dealing with psychoanalysis or with an image which one has of it?

This question, the product both of the divisions which have characterized and continue to characterize the psychoanalytical movement and of the incorporation of Freud's discovery into modern culture, suggests the need for a return to Freud and to what he actually wrote as the most reliable source of information about the psychoanalysis he invented. There, however, a fresh difficulty awaits us. Restricting ourselves to that aspect of analysis which concerns morality, and more precisely moral evil and what determines it, Freud's text needs deciphering. Freud, in fact, did not develop an ethics. Except for certain remarks concerning the severity of the moral code of his own day, he did not draw out the conclusions of his discovery and theory for ethics. It is a common abuse of the truth linked with the appropriation of psychoanalysis by an ideology of emancipation to turn Freud into one of the founders of the "new morality". He puts forward no moral theory because he deals with what precedes and is the basis of all cultural forms including moral theories. Thus, in order to penetrate into what he has to say, it is vital to avoid

45

as far as possible translating, as though they were related to a theory of cultural ethics, expressions and concepts which he uses in connection with his theory of psychoanalysis. Later on we shall see the importance of this observation for the concept of the "super-ego".

When we read Freud it is necessary to abandon all possible preconceptions if the text is to speak for itself. This text, where it is relevant to morality, presents some difficulty. Throughout his research and the occasionally prolific elaboration of his discovery, with characteristic modesty as well as the confidence which comes from knowing he has hit upon the truth, Freud often reveals his uncertainties as well as what he is sure of. This means that nowhere in his finished works do we find a fixed point to guide us. Present-day studies of Freud have yet to throw complete light on the matter. We must therefore limit ourselves to high-lighting certain points, to formulating certain hypotheses to which further study should be devoted with a view to obtaining a really satisfactory account. Precise references to Freud's works have been omitted for reasons of space.

I

For Freud conscience is an effect: the consequence of a renunciation of one's drives. In an essay he wrote in 1930, *Sickness in Civilization* (*Unbehagen in der Kultur*), this theme recurs several times: the human feeling of guilt exists prior to the super-ego and therefore prior to conscience. Freud was certainly not unaware of the existence of a feeling of guilt related to the exercise of conscience: he generally refers to it as "remorse". But this type of conscious guilt does not explain what it takes for granted. Given his theory of psychoanalysis, Freud is led to posit at the base and origin of this guilt, and of conscience, an unconscious feeling, which does not derive from any failure to live up to any moral imperative since it is prior to any such imperative.

This unconscious feeling of guilt is connected with a crime, the "murder of the primordial father" (*Urvater*), one of the principal constituents of the myth first formulated in 1913 in *Totem and Taboo*, which attempted to explain the origins of all cultural forms including religion and morality. It seems likely that

Freud's "prehistoric" event is a basic psychological event in each and every individual, and that it continues to be active precisely in the unconscious. Freud has been accused of constructing a vicious circle: every guilt feeling is determined in relation to a moral law perceived as such. Conscience would therefore be responsible for forbidding "the murder of one's father" and for producing the feeling of guilt which would follow on it. In fact, far from attaching the unconscious feeling of guilt to the transgression of a moral law, Freud goes back beyond this. His reason for locating the origin of the feeling of guilt in the conflict between love and hate for the father (in *Totem and Taboo*) is precisely to escape from the vicious circle, and to posit a basis for it as far back as possible. Whether Freud succeeded entirely in this attempt, and whether his argument depends for its formulation on a specific father-figure still influenced by the effects of rivalry, is a problem which we will not tackle here. We can, however, take our exploration of Freud's contribution a stage further.

The reference he makes to the Oedipus complex shows the direction of his thought. The feeling of guilt arising from the murder presupposes a prior prohibition: the prohibition of incest. The mother is thereby excluded from the arena of desires capable of gratification. Here the father intervenes as the actual representative of the prohibition. Beyond the real father standing for law in the individual's life, beyond the imaginary father fostered by the different human feelings, there is properly speaking the symbolic father who lays down the inescapable law of desire. It is he who forbids access to the mother. The individual therefore finds his path towards unlawful incest blocked by his father. The "murder" of the latter, in so far as he is an obstacle, is the necessary concomitant of the urge to commit incest. Freud would seem to have referred to this murder as if it had been carried out in the flesh in order to indicate that moment in which the symbolical aspect of the prohibition first becomes clear—namely, when the father has ceased to nourish the fantasies representing him as withholding what the individual does not possess. As is quite clear in *Totem and Taboo*, it is the dead father who does the prohibiting.

In the end, Freud seeks to demonstrate that law which is at

the bottom of all laws, which could not as such be inscribed in a
decalogue, a law which, by forbidding desire the immediate
satisfaction which would remove it, marks it with an irremovable
sense of deprivation, and thereby opens up the field it can affect.
Such a law, since it is the very basis of culture, of the entire ordering of speech and of all exchange, is presupposed by any morality.
Neither civilization nor the individual could subsist as such without remaining faithful to the radical sense of deprivation or in-
sufficiency wrought in them by this first prohibition. The dead
father's place must remain unfilled. No mortal man can take it.
Here we have the purpose of the mythical pact between the
brothers in *Totem and Taboo*. But once again it is not a question
of just one moral obligation among others. On the contrary, as
we shall see, all moral obligations only serve to ensure fidelity to
that which at one and the same time explains them and expresses
itself through them.

The unconscious feeling of guilt with which we began is explained by the act of ousting the father in order to take his place;
an act from which none can escape—"original sin", as Freud
called it, linked to the conditions governing each individual's
cultural formation; an act which is at the same time a true disclosure of the primordial prohibition and the deprivation brought
about by it.

One final clarification: the law in question and the desire which
is the occasion for it are unconscious. That is to say, they are
radically inaccessible to the conscious mind. The Oedipus complex of which they form a part should not be treated as a stage
of development which would disappear after having been passed
through. Freud speaks of the Oedipus complex as one which
"succumbs" to repression, which passes into the unconscious.
Whatever difficulty there may be in reconciling Freud's various
remarks on the subject, there is no doubt that for him it is not
disposed of. It remains active in the unconscious. In that respect
it can be said to be of enormous normative importance. It is undoubtedly true that the theory of psychoanalysis seriously under-
mines the foundations of ethics, and thereby the whole question
of moral evil, as we shall see in more detail when we come to the
super-ego and conscience.

II

Freud always made the super-ego, to which he assimilated the conscience, the "inheritor" of the Oedipus complex, to which we referred too briefly above when we examined its role at the origin and foundation of cultural forms. An inheritor is he who takes the place of the dead man. In this case the dead person is the repressed Oedipus and the elements which form an integral part of him, notably the father. It is impossible to speak in Freudian terms of the formation of the conscience without continually being aware of the essential link between the conscience, the super-ego and the prohibition against incest, or, in other words, that which renders the world of desire and communication possible, namely the renunciation of the incestuous drive.

This is not to claim that the link is such that the super-ego merely re-presents this prohibition in a sort of infinite repetition. In fact this link leads us on from an examination of the problem of the foundation to that of the formation, in individuals and groups, of an organ which condenses a whole process. It is in the mechanics of this formation that Freud is above all interested.

He undoubtedly recognizes that external influences govern the child's understanding of right and wrong: the influence of parents and educators in general; threats of the loss of love issued by those with whom the child comes into contact; the influence of the local culture, and so on. But if traces of these external, social influences are recognizable in the super-ego, Freud does not go so far as to make conscience the product of them alone. A basic mechanism intervenes to ensure the internal aspect of the super-ego, namely the individual's identification of himself with the paternal prototype, or else with the parental representative, which marks the decline of the Oedipus complex. In support of this self-identification, which constitutes an inescapable process, the individual acquires something which functions both as an ideal, the ideal of the ego, and as a critical faculty or moral judgment.

It is inaccurate to think of the super-ego as the exact echo in the individual of the ideals and judgments of his parents and the society in which he is brought up. The self-identification referred to also involves the dead father or the father symbol, the one who guarantees, through the prohibition he conveys, the sense of deprivation which safeguards the existence of human order as such. Only in this way can one justify Freud's contention that the super-ego replaces the Oedipus complex. It follows that the greater the degree of identification the more the super-ego shares in the original prohibition. The fact that they are rooted in the unconscious law in this way gives the imperatives of conscience their weight and value. The super-ego ensures a link between this law and the external, parental and social elements. Without the super-ego, the law would not be able to meet the variety of different situations and forms of behaviour. But, without the law, moral commands would lack any justification. When Freud puts the renunciation of one's drives at the origin of conscience it would be more precise to say that it is a question first of all of renouncing the incestuous drive. The renunciations imposed by the individual super-ego and the collective super-ego can then be said to maintain it historically. Since this point was not developed, Freud's theory appears to stress the severe, and even perhaps the cruel aspect of the super-ego. And yet, through the super-ego, by virtue of the distance it maintains between the individual and the unrestrained fulfilment of all his drives, the law keeps its grip on human behaviour.

Two consequences of this renunciation of one's drives imposed by the individual super-ego and the collective super-ego, and recognized by Freud, are here worthy of note: on the one hand the "desexualization" of the erotic urge which is directed towards cultural ends and tends to unite men in love, and on the other, the turning-in on to the individual himself of the aggressive instinct in the form of remorse. We cannot here go into the complex details of Freud's theories of the life instinct and the death instinct. Suffice to note that for Freud the bonds of love between men apparently serve to prevent a violation of the original prohibition and therefore the death of the world of speech and desire. Nevertheless, as aforesaid, the functioning of the conscience is affected by its social origins and by the mechanics of its formation. Freud insisted on many occasions on the severity, aggressiveness and even the sadism, of the super-ego. It is responsible for perpetuating in the individual an intense fear of the loss of love when parental demands are not accepted. It persecutes the individual inasmuch as the aggressive feelings denied direction against those around him turn against himself. It engenders processes of self-punishment discernible even in criminals. All this takes place unknown to the individual, for even if he perceives the prohibitions, he has no idea of the source from which they emanate. The super-ego is, at least in large part, unconscious.

The super-ego is the result and not the cause of suppression and repression. In Freud's view the ego represses drives which worry it. Conscience does not employ this mechanism, the effects of which reverberate on its own level by producing new possibilities, particularly of aggression, which are hidden from the conscious mind. Whatever refinements and nuances should be brought into the discussion at this point, it is possible to declare that, for Freud, conscience, the inheritor of the Oedipus complex, and therefore linked to the unconscious law, is nevertheless a complex entity sensitive to all the influences which have governed and go on governing both its content and its exercise. What is called the voice of conscience not only does not consist of anything innate, but is responsible for issuing imperatives and decrees the origins of which are unknown to the individual and are to be found in an unconscious which, we should remember, may take its bearing from a primary and in some sense structural repression which concerns incestuous desire but is also the effect of secondary repressions occurring at intervals in the life of the individual.

What, then, has Freud to say about moral evil? If evil is determined by the prohibition, and by the feeling of guilt which for the individual goes with the violation of it, then it is true that the inventor of psychoanalysis posited a fault—he even says an "original sin"—inscribed in the Oedipal situation, in his theory of existence. It is fair to say that in his view ultimate evil consists in the transgression of the law which is the basis of all human order. In this sense evil is being unfaithful to the sense of deprivation and, correlatively, good is being faithful to it. The prohibition against failing in respect of this desire for fulfilment can be expressed by the two following correlative vetoes: you shall not possess your mother, you shall not take the place of your father.

This law and its transgression are unconscious. It is truly a question of a law and transgression which are not merely original

but "originating", in the sense that conscience owes its existence
to them. But conscience, which determines what is good and
what is evil, does so not out of practical reasoning, from a perception of what is "reasonable", but under the effect of obscure
influences: the conscious feeling of guilt which leads the individual to speak of moral evil stems from a variety of sources
unknown to the conscious mind.

Is it possible to distinguish in Freud's thought on the subject
different values attached to the imperatives of the super-ego? Is
it possible to visualize a moral evil which, while remaining dependent upon a super-ego, would in some sense be confirmed as
such by an individual assessing it rationally? Freud thinks so, seeing that he attributes a rational mental effort to the ego. However, we should recognize that in his work he merely sketches
the outlines of such an effort. This effort, responsible for weigh-
ing up the different imperatives and for recognizing their sources,
co-existence and organization, is never, as far as he is concerned,
referred to any system of good at all. In the last resort it is regulated by the law and unconscious desire.

All this poses problems for the moralist.

III

Freud's contribution is to throw light on the problem of the
foundations of morality. It is not a question of looking for this
basis in a "human nature" the moral laws of which would make
its demands apparent. It is well known nowadays to what extent
this notion of a regulating nature whose objective requirements
are said to impress themselves on man is held in question. Nor is
it a question of a reason, the cultural relativity of which is increasingly obvious. By locating this basis in the area in which the
passage from nature to culture, from need to desire, from man
to language and speech, is effected, Freud revealed a root basis.
What indeed could be more radical than that without which
there would be no true desire, nor speech, nor communication?
The law cannot but be unconscious in so far as it is necessarily
outside the progression of all cultural forms. One primary in-
junction, a prohibition unformulated in the conscious mind,
underlies all moral discourse. A categorical imperative? Yes and

no. Freud borrows the expression from Kant, but this imperative, the basis of all imperatives, is inscribed in an original situation expressed by the Oedipus complex, through which all must pass because it is basic to being human.

Are we turning full circle to the notion of a moral regulation inherent in human nature? Not at all, because no philosophical or scientific exploration will ever provide us with knowledge of this phenomenon. The prohibition is never determined but determines. It is implied in all cultural developments of any kind.

The question is, how can moral theory do justice to Freud's discovery? This is an open question, posing at the same time the whole problem of the very nature of ethics, starting from new grounds. It is no longer possible, indeed, to think of Freud as being concerned only with neurotic ills and guilt, or with pre-morality, or child morality, alongside which there could supposedly exist, in purified form, a conscious morality with foundations separate from those of "pseudo-morality". His work is, as we have already said, radical. Psychoanalysis must needs be paid tribute in the development of any ethics.

Another conclusion to be drawn from Freudian theory is that the super-ego is not only that which is spoken about, but that which speaks in any determination of right and wrong. It can only speak by expressing itself in terms of its contents and unconscious sources. It does not follow from this that a legislator figure-head is valueless until he has undergone psychoanalysis. But this means that "rational mental effort", to go back to Freud's expression, is indispensable to ensure awareness, organization and coherence in the super-ego's imperatives. Only an approach which is both historical and collective can separate the content and exercise of the super-ego from any bias unknown to the individual concerned.

This is the role of the moralist: precisely to confront, weigh together and organize that which is expressed in the collective super-egos. Space does not here allow for a more detailed, albeit necessary, description, of this role. We should ask ourselves at this juncture whether reference to the ideal love of the Gospel is sufficient.

On this point Freud's theory poses questions for the moralist. It does not indeed put love and its requirements at the heart of morality but, as we have said, a primary prohibition which is quite separate from any of the prohibitions of conscience. Freud does not deny the capital importance of mutual love in human society, but for him the function of this love is to ensure the survival of man, who is constantly threatened by death. Furthermore, this universal love is itself proposed by the ideal which Freud recognizes as one of the functions of the super-ego; an ideal which Freud frequently declared to be devoid of any practical power and effectiveness. Thus, to ensure the existence and growth of those bonds of love he considers necessary for the preservation of culture, Freud relies above all on the presence of *ananké*, the need which forces men to renounce some part of their instinctive gratifications in order to safeguard their life in common by means of the establishment of affective bonds between them.

Such an idea poses the question of the relation between the love of the Gospel and the law, the question of the effectiveness of what is posited as an ultimate moral ideal, and the question of the meaning of a cultural directive which, of its nature, is part of the collective super-ego. Without elaborating on these different points, suffice to say that here there is scope for a love both received and out-going which would be something other than an ideal, and for a grace which would ensure the effectiveness of an impossible command. The possibility of a Christian morality not grounded in the cultural super-ego would not be excluded by the theory of psychoanalysis, provided that what we have termed faithfulness to the deprivation, the renunciation of the incestuous drive, is by the same token faithfulness to the Other, which we name God the Father.

The notion of "sublimation" is brought in by Freud to attempt to explain the process by which drives which forsake immediate gratification become re-directed towards higher cultural satisfactions. Here we have a transformation which has nothing to do with any conscious efforts and which, in Freudian theory, can be explained only by acceptance of deprivation, by entry into the initial renunciation required by the law. But this entry is not opened up by efforts to conform to an ideal which always bears the marks of the super-ego. By introducing the concept of sublimation into his theory, Freud clearly demonstrates, though only by brief remarks, that morals as a body of laws to which man should submit remains open-ended, open on to something it does not itself procure, namely the transformation, heightening and universalization of drives.

At least we can now state that the problem of the relation between the theory of psychoanalysis and ethics is something other than a problem of the frontiers between two disciplines. The introduction of psychoanalysis into scientific thought poses a question other than that of the frontiers or the limits to be assigned to it. It is a question of a violation of the border-line, with implications relevant to all cultural forms. If the truth—or one dimension of the truth—is revealed by psychoanalysis, then this invasion is justified. It remains true, none the less, as Freud says, that men are not particularly disposed to accept it.

Translated by Jonathan Cavanagh

Norbert Schiffers

Guilt and Moral Evil in the Light of the Study of Behaviour

IF WE want to use the findings of the study of behaviour for a practical approach to the abstract theological notion of guilt, there are a few points to be settled first.

I

An increasing number of psychotherapists refer somewhat sharply and so perhaps a little short-sightedly to what they call an "ecclesiogenic (i.e., church-bred) neurosis".[1] By this they mean the kind of neurosis brought about by rigid moral doctrine and the preaching about sin which goes with it. To prove to themselves that it is useful to stand the strain implied in the faith, Christians like to talk about the inevitable guilt from which God alone can set us free. For them this argument is easily backed by reference to the fifth petition of the Our Father (Matt. 6. 12). But when we read on and include the second part of that petition, we are at once faced with the mission to turn the life of the Christian community into a visible sign of this presence of God's forgiveness (Acts 4. 32; 1 John 3. 14).[2] And once the Christian has understood that, he has to explain to himself how we can sensibly talk about men forgiving each other. As we shall see, the study of behaviour offers a handful of ready answers.

[1] E. Schaetzing, "Die ecclesiogenen Neurosen", in *Wege zum Menschen,* 7 (1955), pp. 97 f.
[2] H. Harsch, *Das Schuldproblem in Theologie und Tiefenpsychologie* (Heidelberg, 1965), pp. 44 f.

If, therefore, we want to make use of these answers, this does not mean that we wish to dispense with the preaching of God's forgiveness through salvation. To put the theological concept of guilt so completely aside would simply emasculate man's experience of guilt altogether. This would in any case be unscientific and could not therefore be the condition of a science like the study of behaviour. As the two parts of the fifth petition of the Our Father show, the point is rather to see the monolithic, over-all notion of guilt as comprising the whole complex reality contained in guilt, and to take it again so seriously that its components can be studied separately without doing harm to its unity.

Before we deal with the question of method, we must mention a fact which has become almost a general assumption because of the way the exact sciences have treated the problem of guilt but which has a consoling aspect for us men beset with guilt. At one time some too hastily progressive thinkers almost overlooked the phenomenon of guilt, and some of the pioneers of psychotherapy, sociology, and the study of behaviour already foresaw a kind of optimism leading to a tendency to consider it possible to dispose totally of the problem of guilt if only it were approached rationally. Today such a view, far too utopian and contradicted by fact, is held by only few behaviourists.[3]

Theologians are not alone in pointing to the obstructive aspect of guilt, and neither are they dependent for support only on philosophers who speak of "existential guilt" because man is responsible only to himself.

This support was in any case always problematic because of the practical question whether and how man will come to his true selfhood in his concrete existence, and therefore can ever be set free from this existential guilt.

But if today psychologists, sociologists and students of

[3] For the theory of behaviourism, see Dollard, Doob, Miller, Mowrgr, and Sears, *Frustration and Aggression* (New Haven, 1939); T. Parsons, *Sozialstruktur und Persönlichkeit* (Frankfurt, 1969). For the objections to it: K. Lorenz, *Das sogennante Böse. Zur Naturgeschichte der Aggression* (6th edn., Vienna, 1964); R. Dahrendorf, *Gesellschaft und Freiheit* (Munich, 1961); A. Mitscherlich, "Aggression—Spontaneität—Gehorsam", in *Bis hierher und nicht weiter. Ist die menschliche Aggression unbefriedbar?*, ed. by A. Mitscherlich (Munich, 1969), pp. 66 f.

behaviour are more than ever concerned with finding a viable therapy for the anxiety created by guilt, then their findings are not only helpful for the interpretation of the theological concept of guilt but even point in that direction because of the carefully delimited and therefore exact way in which they formulate the questions, and so already indicate that the problem of guilt, by its very complexity, cannot be solved by any single science.

All scientists, even the behaviourists, agree that, as a human burden, guilt can no longer be ignored as a phenomenon of human conduct. When this burden becomes oppressive, it leads to uncontrollable outbreaks, and this means that there is some connection between guilt and aggressiveness.

While this connection is basic to the thinking of psychologists, sociologists, and students of behaviour, it does not settle the problem of guilt, nor does it leave the theologian in the cold with his preoccupation with man's guilt, but demands of both scientists and theologians a convincing understanding of the meaning of guilt, which, as "aggression", plays a part in man's existential behaviour.

If theologians and empirical scientists are to work together on these lines, the next step must be to elucidate the meaning of "aggression" in connection with what we call "guilt".

Freud pointed out that within his model of the human psyche, in which he distinguished between the ego, the id, and the super-ego, the empirically observable feelings of guilt indicate a tension between these three levels of the psyche. The punishment-threatening super-ego in man[4] dips into the unconscious and sees there, in that reservoir of urges that is designated by the id, certain impulses which the ego, with its thought, observation, memory, its combining and guiding functions, does not know of because of its repression mechanism. The undesirable result of this knowledge of the super-ego, which the ego does not possess, is that the super-ego sets itself up as judge and with increasing severity and rigidity pronounces the ego guilty of those unconscious urges. As a consequence, the ego which, with its human functions of thought, assimilation, and so on, should behave responsibly, feels itself guilty but does not know of what.

This highly unsatisfactory situation of the ego is not only suffi-

[4] S. Freud, *Ges. Werke* (London, 1966), XV, pp. 64 f.

ciently well known by statistics, it also explains the reactions of scrupulous and neurotic people and even the transference rituals by which the unknown guilt is transferred to scapegoats that must be sent into the desert, whipped, or even killed, in order to get rid of the guilt which we have thus shifted from our own shoulders.

Although one welcomes such explanations provided by Freud's structural model for the analysis and therapy of types of illness and "sacrificial actions" that are not or are only poorly human-ized, they do not give us a universally valid solution of the prob-lem of guilt, as Freud may have thought.

This first became clear in the treatment of psychoses, which Freud still thought was impossible. When it was realized that a practically uninhibited commitment of love could break through the communication barriers of the schizophrenic, it was also realized "that sexuality is not the basis of love, but the other way round".[5]

This insight into the importance of interpersonal action drove the theory of psychoanalysis already fundamentally in the direc-tion of social relationships,[6] and it became vital to seek a closer link between these relationships and the patterns statistically established by the study of psychosomatic illnesses. Since this study investigates internal, and therefore also urge-motivated, impulses *via* bodily expressions of conduct, the study of behaviour was brought into the search for a broader solution of the problem of guilt which has become so important in psychotherapy.[7]

Bodily expressions of behaviour that can be observed have shown that the foundations of animal and human conduct also comprise those early impressions which cannot be repressed without guilt.

Freud already saw that the major urges must be understood as unsatisfied "radical" urges, ready to be fulfilled, combining to-gether and producing an almost violent energy. If we want to

[5] A. Sborowitz, *Der leidende Mensch* (Düsseldorf, 1960), p. 67.

[6] E. H. Erikson, "The Problem of Ego-Identity", in *Psychological Issues,* ed. by G. Klein (New York, 1959); D. Rapaport, "The Structure of Psycho-analytical Theory", in *Psychology. A Study of Science*, 1/3, ed. by S. Koch (New York, 1959).

[7] A. Mitscherlich, *Über etablierte Unfreiheiten im Denken der un-bewussten Freiheit. Krankheit als Konflikt* (Frankfurt, 1966), pp. 100 f.

canalize the energy which bursts from these combined urges, and is thus released, so that the fulfilment mechanisms of man, to which we give the name "consciousness", can become viable, and if we want to guide it to a responsible conservation of life in socially bearable or even desirable ways, then we can no longer put our trust simply in a "goodness" of nature which will do all this by itself, and therefore without relation to the group.[8] On the contrary, we should very carefully observe, describe, and learn to understand the causal connections of the two factors which influence the required adjustment, namely, the tensions which spring from the need created by the urges, and the compulsion and aid which work on it from the outside.

If we want to achieve this, we can no longer limit ourselves to theological reflection upon the complete wholeness of organic systems such as we find them in animals and human beings. We will not be satisfied with aesthetic references to the beauty of a nature which has already accomplished all that is required.

Such an isolated morphological reflection is not enough for the understanding and management of life—no more than the blind confidence in a culture which, for man, replaces the natural instinct that guides the animal, and which we would simply have to shape in the continuing history of mankind. Nor can we call the price for the "openness" of this human culture simply a time-bound "debt" of man, as A. Gehlen and others have done.[9]

Neither the suggestion that man has fallen behind his technological inventions, nor the confidence that man will catch up through his cultural drive, if "nature" will only give him time, are tenable when we look at the findings of the study of behaviour.

This behaviour study has no doubt shown that little children only need time to pass from the suckling stage to feeding themselves with the help of a spoon. To feed oneself one needs neither to study nor to exercise responsibility, and yet it comes about gradually as a cultural action.

But if we relied on this process in adolescence or even in adult-

---

[8] S. Freud, op. cit., XV, pp. 102 f. and 110; A. Mitscherlich, Bis hierher und nicht weiter . . . , pp. 66–103.

[9] A. Gehlen, Anthropologische Forschung (Hamburg, 1961); A. Portmann, Zoologie und das neue Bild des Menschen (Hamburg, 1956).

hood, we would neglect the learning process which becomes necessary later on, and would base our view of the growth of culture on a childish pattern which would be nothing but irresponsible and romantic child-play.

Because technical development changes the human condition much more quickly than the evolutionary passage from one behaviour pattern to another, the appreciation of the lag in our natural cultural development always ends in that pessimism which sees man, and his difficulty in adjusting himself, as a "backward machine". If we understand the reality of a world which threatens to lose its way, we cannot rest content with singing the praises of a cultural progress which we constantly fail to achieve.

Social responsibility for the human community will force us to take the trouble accurately to observe the threatening process of the interchange of energy so that we can pin it down accurately by induction and in the end control it. The social and ethical responsibility for a culpable breakdown in man's cultural progress is the reason why depth psychology and study of behaviour do not examine the ways in which aggression works theologically but rather with the help of an inductive analysis of the causes.[10] The study of behaviour is a science, not a manual for meditation.

Through its scientific character, behaviour study is linked with depth psychology and sociology in so far as these sciences bring a formal scientific approach to this analysis of the causes. Because of this methodical approach these three modern sciences are not world-views to suit some ideology but sciences in the strict sense of the word.

As sciences they respect guilt as a pressing and oppressive reality in man, a reality which has not fallen out of the sky as an inevitable fate but has been caused by failures for which man is responsible and which man therefore has to tackle responsibly with the help of an analysis of the causes. The theologian is therefore not the only one to maintain that guilt is not a fate but a fact for which we are responsible and which must be tested with the data provided by the study of behaviour.

[10] K. Lorenz, *Vom Weltbild des Verhaltensforschers* (Munich, 1968), pp. 11 f. and 97 f.

II

That there is such a thing as "aggression" is the common experience of us all. Anybody with a little sense of responsibility knows that these destructive impulses aimed at members of the species must be tackled by powers that are stronger and organized. The ordinary man does not find it particularly helpful to leave this grappling with the evil in his fellow men to some superman, whether detective, sheriff, or some individual bursting with feelings for humanity. Even the preaching of a God who will judge evil-doers at the end of time only affects man's history if people let themselves be moved to obey the good.

In order to obey in this way man will have to pass from the fear of punishment which regulates his conduct initially to the wise view that, as the image of God, he is in duty bound to imitate the good God and to act as his representative in the historical process. But when this imitation is tried out it leads to the experience that it cannot be achieved without the acceptance of suffering. Here one can read up the examples given in books of behaviour study that have become common literature. The most comprehensive source for this, and without the professional jargon, is certainly K. Lorenz's best-seller, *Das so-genannte Böse* (The so-called Evil).

I will not repeat here what can be read elsewhere because this still does not answer our question about the interpretation of moral evil by the students of behaviour. In order to make any progress in this field we have to ask a third question with which this study of behaviour is certainly familiar. It concerns the "adjustment value" of a given form of behaviour. The student of this value would, for instance, like to know what kind of profit people derive from war, cruelty, malicious mischief, and other such hateful misdeeds.

On the other hand, it is also valuable to find out what the "adjustment value" is of the conduct of those who prefer to suffer injustice rather than do it.

To find the answer for the first group, whom, for brevity's sake and without any moral connotation, we shall call "evil", the psychiatrists have provided us with so many illustrations that the courts already have whole volumes of them.

If we take the trouble not merely to read these but to try to assess them, we come to the frightening, because socially dangerous conclusion that many of those people who have committed acts against their fellow men and are rightly threatened with punishment for the protection of both individuals and society at large, have acted in a repressive condition in which they were no longer morally responsible. If we go by ethical norms, these people, who spread calamity, cannot be called "evil", if we can establish what a condition of uncontrolled urges is.

If we take into account here that the term "urge" only refers to a working hypothesis which allows us to differentiate and therefore to understand more clearly various given kinds of human conduct,[11] we can still only very generally describe the condition of uncontrolled urges of people who suffer from destructive compulsions as an uncontrolled activity of these people, which has broken out.

This general description of the condition as "uncontrolled activity" is in fact so general that it applies also to the "good" people we mentioned above, those who suffer injustice rather than do it. In their case, too, the active endurance of a threatening, and perhaps ultimately fatal, situation can be described with reference to an activity which is not checked by consideration of the preservation of the species or by the duty of self-preservation as dictated by the benefit of the community. As has been said: a dead soldier may be a hero, but he is no longer useful.

This holds even when we look at the Christian opposite of this sentence: the blood of the martyrs is the seed of Christianity. For this Christian maxim is also clearly dictated by the highly beneficial value of the deed for a group of people.

In other words, the adjustment value of a human act must be assessed in every case by two interdependent constitutive elements, which we can describe as the powerful root-urge of "aggressiveness" on the one hand, and the "beneficial effect on the community" on the other.

This useful description as such is neither an insult to nor a

---

[11] S. Freud, op. cit., XV, p. 101: "Die Trieblehre ist sozusagen unsere Mythologie". For the development of this teaching about urges as a theory into a working hypothesis, see H. Kunz, Die Aggressivität und die Zärtlichkeit (Bern, 1946), p. 48, and A. Mitscherlich, op. cit., pp. 94–6.

demolition of an ideal value system which presents community-building actions as morally good. But one has to admit that this description means to provide an enlightened criticism of moral threats, implying sanctions which do not correspond to the ideal of people who act in a morally good way and who see in this ideal a value system.

We have therefore to ask how this human resistance can be prevented from being reduced to cowardice by the exercise of psycho-social power, which, as we know, can also operate in unpleasantly dictatorial ways and become truly aggressive without any control. In order to avoid these abuses of a social pressure which can make even the noblest ideal degenerate into a mere ideology, we need, among other things, a critical understanding of the value of the use of action if we want to have a norm for the ideal situation in connection with aggressiveness and social benefit.

Thanks to the fieldwork undertaken by J. Huxley,[12] students of behaviour were able to arrive at extensive conclusions with regard to the phenomenon of "ritualization". It was shown that ritual behaviour among animals and humans originated in those activities which are connected with partnering and breeding activities that serve the survival of the species, not the destruction of it.

Thus, for example, feeding from beak to beak developed into the greeting ceremonial of kissing, which still looks like feeding from mouth to mouth but has become a ritual gesture. This gesture not only relieves a potentially aggressive situation but creates a bond against any destructive aggression that may threaten the partners or the group from outside.

Another example is the well-known "de-lousing" process monkeys indulge in. Originally this was a cleaning operation and part of an aspect of parental care during the breeding season. Among the large animals it is no more than a friendly gesture from one member of the species to another; he asks for it in the nicest possible way, and so shows himself in need of help.

What looks like a search for food or giving of food became ritualized into a form of conduct which no longer served the

[12] J. Huxley, *Man in the Modern World* (London, 1947).

purpose of the original biological activities but took over the function of controlling the urge of destructive aggressiveness.

The same thing holds for the clinging together required by two members of the species for their sexual partnership. Here ritualization changed the function into a form of conduct which expresses togetherness and the will not to do each other any harm. Such behaviour, then, at a dance or some other form of togetherness has nothing to do with a pan-sexual interpretation of human self-giving, nor does it necessarily lead to intercourse.

Such and similar forms of ritualization are rather to be understood as socially and ethically valuable expressions of adjustment of activities that originate in the historical development of the instinct and are originally biological and potentially uncontrollable. Such a ritualization becomes control of aggressiveness. Ritualization, then, protects one partner against a fellow member of the species with a powerful inclination to devour his partner.

These observations of the historical development of ritualization bring us, from the point of view of scientific theory, some methodologically sound information because they fulfil the three conditions for proceeding in an inductive and consequential way in the study of behaviour.

The process of ritualization has been observed not only among organic creatures of the same species, but also among those that belong to a closely related species or even those that are phylogenetically far distant from each other. But this means that in ritualization we are dealing with some general kind of law which cannot be overlooked when we talk about controlling factors. Whole series of observation experiments have shown the hypothesis that ritualized behaviour has adjustment value in that it civilizes unruly urges, to have clearly assumed a measure of probability which we can take into account.

Beyond this fact that we can rely on the restraining effects of ritualization on aggressiveness, we may also be encouraged by the observation that we have here a re-direction of those functions that are indispensable to the preservation of the species.

If this is so, then ritualization brings about something that we have known about for some time in what is called the taboo. It is not only that, as in the case of boxers, fairness is ensured by certain regions of the body or ways of hitting being taboo to both contestants. Behaviour study is familiar with numerous other ways in which this taboo code shows control mechanisms that check forms of attack which might injure the body in special cases where the contestant exposes unprotected nakedness. That is why, for instance, bony fish and fallow buck never take advantage of the side, exposed in order to show off, in their duels, and why swaggering adolescents start their aggressive jostling by digging the elbow into the much better protected narrow sides of the body. This natural observation of the taboo code does not, in these cases, re-direct or transform the blow that will do real injury, but it nevertheless brings in a restraint.

Now, if we hold, as Christianity and all higher forms of ethics do, that deliberate injury to the body, uncontrolled sexuality, or the exploitation of weak self-surrender, are not only actions to be rejected, but also dangerous manifestations of evil, then the interpretation of such evidence by the study of behaviour leads us to some fundamental theses:

1. If ritualization and taboo do not destroy the aggressive urge but re-direct or restrain it, then we have here a pointer to the fact that this urge has two functions, one to preserve life and one to destroy it.

2. Biologically speaking there is much to be said for the thesis that love can turn into hate when, in the case of a frustrated human being, the ritualized re-direction or the restraining mechanism of the taboo no longer functions.

3. If instinctive good and aggressive evil are as close as life and death, then even man can make the biochemical attempt to use a selective breeding process in order to let the preserving tendencies in the basic urges prevail over the destructive ones.

4. This suggestion about human breeding is opposed by responsible scientists, not merely by a consent based on an unspoken taboo, but on the ground of a deeper insight into the motivation of this taboo. Of the two most important insights here, the first is that the preservation of the species is always a conservative mechanism, which is not bad in itself. Yet, the impulse to act, which is a necessary aspect of the basic urge, might well lead the breeder, guided by increasing knowledge, to a dominant position over men that are only guided by their natural

experience, and thus set up a structure of superior power over others that then become dependent.

This, however, means that the inequality between those guided by science and those limited to experience would be maintained, or—as is rather to be expected—the frustration of those led by natural experience will make them susceptible and only too ready for aggression. But this conduct will create a reaction in those that control the superior breeding process, and make them equally susceptible. The result would then be that the whole process becomes a vicious circle of mutually pursued aggressiveness.

The second insight, which goes against the building up of the widest possible control mechanisms, has direct normative value. People discover the control mechanisms by experience. But if, for our judgment of fellow humans, we only believe in our own experiences, we will make a mistake in judgment which does not do justice to them. By experience a man who is looking for a partner may be inclined to fall for any woman with a "baby face" because such an outward appearance stirs the maternal or paternal instinct. Then any candidate who is much better educated but has a less babyish face will always draw the shortest straw. This does not do justice either to her or the gravity of the matter. Purely instinctive choices always lead to resentment.

5. This last example brings the current interpretation of evil in behaviour study under the critical judgment of that interpersonal phenomenon which we call social control. This is not just a matter of instincts and experiences. It only comes into its own in the conscious manipulation of the relationship between facts that are scientifically established. We must not only be informed about the way these facts hang together, but we also have to learn what to do with the available information. We will not discover this if we only look at the biological laws by which behaviour study is bound.

We shall have to become more fully aware of the structures that underlie communication, of the conclusions reached by the psychological study of the learning process, of ecumenical pressures and many other things, so that morally responsible behaviour can turn our instinctive actions, prompted initially by the aggressive urge, into forces that work for human progress.

6. This use of the aggressive urge has already been pushed into

the foreground in behaviour study by the analysis of the ritual-
izing actions, which the uninitiated still look on as manifestations
of evil. The sober scientist, intent on finding a solution, recognizes, however, that to describe ritual behaviour as "so-called
evil" does not explain it away. For evil does not appear as a
natural force in either the biological, or the didactic, or the
social-economic process, but arises in the spirit of man when he
goes against the insights contained in the context of related facts
and against the less self-centred application of knowledge thus
acquired.

7. When students of behaviour reckon with the fact that "one
cannot implicitly rely on the control mechanisms",[13] they do not
neutralize evil, but bring to it the knowledge that bodily actions
are not evil, and this is more in harmony with human dignity.
The devil does not live in our body, but "deceives" the spirit of
man.

If the findings of behaviour study are still modest in so far as
evil in its social ethical aspect is concerned, they nevertheless
help us to overcome the dualism implied in a still widespread
hostile attitude to the body.

[13] K. Lorenz, op. cit., p. 186.

Translated by Theo Westow

Wilhelm Korff

Dilemmas of a "Guilt-Free Ethic"

THE crisis in ethics is by no means restricted to questions of material content. Every attempt, therefore, to alleviate it merely by radical change in the sphere of moral norms ends up by being the sort of therapy that is content to stop short at treating symptoms. It is in fact quite clear that the contemporary moral crisis is far more involved than any mere questioning of the traditional stock of norms. Its centre really lies far more in the field of structures. It is concerned with those categories which form the boundaries within which alone morality was, up till now, operative and was experienced.

The new critique of the phenomenon of guilt argues at precisely this structural level. It is, at least in part, a truly radical critique, but it is impelled by a serious human concern, and it is this that gives it its special character. It has three main fundamental reservations to make about the traditional ethics of guilt; these correspond to the different starting-points and intentions of the different arguments:

(a) The traditional outlook depends on an understanding of conscience that cripples the driving force of the human personality, of man's deepest Self.

(b) It exists in a state of interior interdependence with a social structure that blocks all effective development towards a more human world.

(c) It is so deeply bound up with its ethos that it shows itself in general to be archaic and pre-rational.

I. THE REBELLION OF THE SELF

"Does the proof of your guilt not lie in your punishment?"—
thus argues the chaplain in André Gide's dramatic rendering of
Kafka's *The Trial*. "You must see your error and convince yourself that 'I am being punished, therefore I am guilty'."[1] This
pointed non-sequitur undoubtedly crystallizes and takes to their
logical conclusion tendencies whose seed has been laid right at
the psychological heart of the experience of guilt, in the moment
of *accusation* itself. So it is that A. Hesnard's small programmatic
book *Morale sans peché*[2] seems from the methodological point
of view to be entirely justified. In accordance with his particular
psychological starting-point, he makes this factor of accusation
the key to his critical analysis of the guilt phenomenon; and it
follows from this that guilt (theologically "sin") is rooted and
constituted in the mode of interaction that is defined by the judge-
defendant relationship. This goes for guilt in its social form as
well as in its interior form of self-accusation and self-imputation.
Thus the "world under the sign of guilt" shows itself necessarily
as a nexus of that interaction in which man is the accuser of man,
or is accused by him, in which he is hangman or victim, and for
the most part both together. And it is precisely this life-in-
common, dominated by aggression and fear, lived under the sign
of guilt, that according to Hesnard makes the world a "world
sick with sin"[3]—a world that prevents man from really accepting
and answering for himself and to his neighbour, and from giving
and experiencing love, community and protection.

The governing force in this "world sick with sin" is essentially
an ethic which, borne along on a ground-current of fear, spends
all its forces in a purely negative, defensive campaign against
possible losses in the sphere of social and individual integrity.
Guilt-ethics means living in a network of sanctions; it means

[1] Quoted from J. Lacroix, *Le sens de l'athéisme moderne* (Tournai,
1958).
[2] Published Paris, 1954. This small book systematizes and carries on a
train of thought begun in Hesnard's work *L'univers morbide de la faute*
(Paris, 1949).
[3] Hesnard, the doctor and psychologist, sees this as giving rise to a
necessary inner connection between sin and illness. Illness is in the final
analysis "existence in a world of guilt".

regimentation of one's being, neutralization of one's impulses, frustration of one's driving force. And all this, according to Hesnard, produces a mental climate where the person is always willing to adapt, to conform and to subordinate himself in a way that allows all personal responsibility to degenerate. Where this moral outlook is presupposed, man's existence is hemmed in with inexorable, inescapable sanctions, and against them his life can be wrecked. There is no way out but to turn all his aggression back onto himself: the failure of the ethic is taken back inside him, and it installs itself inside him as *bad conscience*.

Nietzsche, in his day, had already laid bare these roots of "bad conscience". It grows out of the relentless legalism of that collective domestication of man which, constraining and breaking his native driving-force and instincts, throws them back within him to turn against his own Self. He used words quite as sharp and cutting as ours: "This instinct of freedom forced into being latent . . . this instinct of freedom forced back, trodden back, imprisoned within itself, and finally only being able to find vent and relief in itself; this, only this, is the beginning of the 'bad conscience'."[4] This socio-psychological analysis exposes in a consistent fashion the *repressive* structures that are undoubtedly present in the "bad conscience"—structures whose trail can be pursued right back to the roots of the genesis of conscience, and which, with their own peculiar set of rules, are capable of engendering a whole culture of life-denying, guilt-ridden "vivisections of conscience"[5] in the "soul whose will is cloven in two within itself".[6] Only against the background of these structures can the elemental protests of both Nietzsche and Hesnard be understood. Their voices are raised against that religious, sacralizing legitimation of the "guilt complex", which only serves to consolidate the *status quo*. Their atheism, too, expresses their unconditional refusal to accept "the 'Lord', the 'Father', the Sire, the Beginning of the world";[7] and it protests against all attempts to substitute an all-embracing guilt-context round mankind, along the lines of original sin. At its deepest core this atheism aims at

[4] F. Nietzsche, "The Genealogy of Morals", in *The Complete Works of F. Nietzsche* (Edinburgh, 1910–13), vol. 13, p. 104, translated by H. Samuel.
   [5] *Ibid.*, p. 116.   [6] *Ibid.*, p. 105.   [7] *Ibid.*, p. 112.

no more and no less than a radical rehabilitation of the freedom and dignity of man.[8]

In their understanding of their own position, those who propose this moral outlook purged of "guilt complexes" do of course consider as decisive the fact that they see liberation from the forces of repression and restraint not in any way as a total and entire abolition of guilt feelings, but essentially as a process that changes very basically the way in which these feelings have been stressed. Hesnard sees this re-accentuation as vouched for in the release of the "bad conscience" from the prison of inwardness and constant self-reference into the liberating field of interpersonal responsibility and life "for one another". Nietzsche sees it in the transition from conformity to non-conformity. For him the road to freedom begins at the point where man breaks the bonds of subordination and ceases to connect "bad conscience" with rebellion against repressive ideals; at the point, therefore, where, instead of regarding his "natural proclivities with an 'evil eye' ",[9] he associates his guilt feelings with the *denial* of his instinct for life. What becomes clear from all this is that the protagonists of this "guilt-free ethic" are concerned to criticize an understanding of guilt that seems to block the way to a more creative and more human life; they are not concerned to criticize away the phenomenon of guilt altogether—a fact which absolves them not least from the all-too-naïve reproach of nihilism.[10]

These attempts to grasp the meaning of guilt do no doubt contain much good sense, and they continually open up new aspects of the problem. But the decisive question remains: does the shift they intend to bring about in the understanding of guilt feelings assure the development of a properly qualified moral outlook?

---

[8] A characteristic feature of modern atheism is evident here. There is clearly far more stress on ethical than on epistemological argumentation. It is a "postulated atheism" (M. Müller), springing entirely from the idea of freedom as the condition and basis of being oneself, of making oneself —the condition on which man radically depends if he is to come of age. Marxism (up to and including A. Schaff, R. Garaudy and C. Luporini), existentialism (Sartre) and even idealism (N. Hartmann) reach agreement with Nietzsche at this point.

[9] Nietzsche, *loc. cit.*, p. 116.

[10] Nietzsche does indeed see his "man of the future", the "conqueror of God and of Nothingness" as "Antichrist", but also essentially as "Antinihilist". *Ibid.*, p. 117.

It is a shift which implies in principle the dissolution of what Huxley calls the "proto-ethical mechanism"[11] of an authority-determined, society-regulating conception of conscience. The question has no easy answer. For although Nietzsche and Hesnard do advocate an "insubordination of conscience" as the enduring ferment-point of human freedom in the face of constrictive norm-structures, neither of them considers that he has thereby run the whole gamut of that freedom within which the new moral outlook he postulates is realized. Freedom does not mean for them regression to an unformed, "natural" existence, liberated from all external "claims", governed by instinct alone. It does not mean that at all. What it essentially means is existence which in transcending the mould of norms cast round it, reaches to and finds the real potentialities of its being. For Hesnard this takes place in the creative turning of one person to another; for Nietzsche in the emancipation of the individual into radical acceptance of sovereign self-responsibility. Nietzsche quite explicitly draws out this line of argument when he conceives the formation of the *autonomous conscience* as the "ripest fruit", the outcome positively aimed at, of that "colossal process" in which man was collectively tamed and made calculable with the help of the "morality of custom" (*Sittlichkeit der Sitte*). At the end of this process, surpassing it and relegating it to the order of a means, stands the radically sovereign individual—the individual who, in this moment of "proud knowledge" that he has won freedom and power "over himself and over fate", first gains for himself his own personal *responsibility*.[12]

With this autonomous, self-possessing conscience, however, Nietzsche finally establishes the possibility of a moral consciousness that no longer needs to lean continually on the prop of collective norm structures. And in doing so he goes in principle well beyond the position of those moral psychologists like S. Freud, and even more clearly A. Gehlen, who see the whole of moral culture, including its autonomous developments, as subject to permanent control by the tribunal of social norms and institutions. In Freud's theory, for example, every liberation of the ego from the social controls which internalize themselves in the

[11] J. Huxley, *Essays of a Humanist* (London, 1964), p. 110.
[12] Nietzsche, *loc. cit.*, pp. 63-4.

super-ego, appears as a liberation of the libido which, repressed by those controls, is positively open to sublimation. It is a liberation which cannot but throw man back to a pre-rational level, delivering him up to a self-destruction that is at once cultural and moral.[13] Gehlen's position is similar. He sees man as an "undetermined" being, condemned by nature to exile in the school of culture. So for him, any dismantling of institutions whose precise function it is to transform man's immediate impulses into responsible modes of thought and action freed from the burdensome demands of decision, must lead necessarily and naturally to the brink of degeneration. And this is a threat to man's moral stability.[14]

The particular weakness of these latter theories clearly lies in their playing down of subjectivity so completely that along with it that very tribunal of appeal is outlawed, which alone could support a conscience that was capable of being "insubordinate" and was critical of norms. In fact nobody else considers it profitable to argue at this level at all, except those like Wilhelm Reich, or more recently Arno Plack,[15] who see the panacea for the ills

[13] Cf. here especially S. Freud, *Das Unbehagen in der Kultur*. Freud sees all culture as based on renunciation of the instinctual drives and postponement of immediate gratification: "Individual freedom is not good, so far as culture is concerned."

[14] Cf. A. Gehlen, *Der Mensch, Seine Natur und seine Stellung in der Welt* (Bonn, [5]1955); also *Urmensch und Spätkultur* (Bonn, 1956); also *Anthropologische Forschung* (Hamburg, 1961); also *Studien zur Anthropologie und Soziologie* (Neuwied, Berlin, 1963). Even if Gehlen, with his thesis that man is the "not yet firmly established animal" (cf. *Der Mensch, loc. cit.*, p. 10), does take over a formula of Nietzsche's, he does not follow Nietzsche to the logical conclusion that man is a prospecting, constantly self-liberating, "responsible" being. And Gehlen is everything but an "evolutionist" in the way he rejects as "blind alleys" (cf. *Studien, loc. cit.*, p. 190) the very questions about "origins" that are so characteristic of Nietzsche. For Gehlen the possibility of subjectively responsible activity is bound far more to *institutions*. These institutions *relieve man of a great burden* and so allow room for the development of subjectivity. But in a sort of tragic circle, this subjectivity no longer takes the form of a functional means of living, but fills itself up with its own worth, and, making itself its own goal, ends up in a state of hypertrophy.

[15] W. Reich, *Die Funktion des Orgasmus. Zur Psychopathologie und zur Soziologie des Geschlechtslebens* (Leipzig, Vienna, Zürich, 1927); also *Einbruch der Sexualmoral* (Leipzig, Vienna, Zürich, 1931); A. Plack, *Die Gesellschaft und das Böse. Eine Kritik der herrschenden Moral* (Munich, 1967, [5]1969). Both authors imply a causal relationship between suppression

of individual and social life as lying in the destruction of all normativity and the consequent liberation of the instincts *as such*. They are, then, the only ones who can be reached by the arguments these theories propose.

Nietzsche's idea of conscience, on the other hand, certainly leads on to a constructive subjectivity. But there is something deeply suspicious about the radical way he hypostatizes in the form of "will for power" the freedom that comes into being through this conscience. Beyond the saving reach of any further faculty of reason, the "will for power" has made this freedom its own prisoner.[16] The result is a moral outlook which, in the measure that it frees itself from the objective bonds of the "morality of custom", puts into practice for its own part directives that bring man's actions into a no less brutal custody, and does so in the name of a subjectivity which has been delivered up to itself.

The question that arises from all this, then, directly concerns the moral autonomy which through the course of history has grown to be man's lot. Is it at all possible in this state of affairs to have a moral outlook which so reconciles *freedom* and *normativity* that moral autonomy can and will grow to maturity? And that there, elevated above all thought of depravity, it will no longer be in need of repression? That is the question that has stimulated H. Marcuse more than anyone else to look for the social and psychological laws and conditions of operation of a *non*-repressive and yet *rationally* instinctive morality.[17] Such a morality would free man as "conscious rational subject"[18] so that he could come of age into a state of "self-sublimation".[19] This state would lead him beyond the blind bonds of traditionally

---

of sexual instincts and aggressive social behaviour. Plack opposes behaviourist ideas (Lorenz, Portmann) when he sees aggression as a secondary, "learnt" configuration of instincts which disappears of itself with the resolution of sexual taboos.

[16] And cf. the section "Redemption", in "Thus Spake Zarathustra", *The Complete Works of F. Nietzsche*, vol. 11, pp. 165–71, translated by T. Common. "Will—so is the emancipator and joy-bringer called: thus have I taught you, my friends! But now learn this likewise: the Will itself is still a prisoner." *Ibid.*, p. 168.

[17] H. Marcuse, *Eros and Civilization* (Boston, 1955); also *One Dimensional Man* (Boston, 1964).

[18] *Eros and Civilization*, loc. cit., p. 150.   [19] *Ibid.*, p. 207.

ordered moral conduct, and beyond the pseudo-humanitarian claims of a production-geared society which, governed only by the law of economic effectiveness, aims all the more at keeping him in tutelage as a needy, and so manipulable and marketable, commodity.[20] Marcuse begins by saying that this state of affairs is by no means inevitable; indeed it can be revoked in principle, for it is an historical phenomenon within the process of change in social consciousness and social structure. And he goes on to say that the high degree of productivity achieved by modern culture and civilization under the iron fist of the "performance principle" is itself basically a first necessary step, but a substantial and decisive one, towards the development of a culture of non-alienated work and of non-repressive sublimation of the instincts: a culture that will, of course, go on to surpass qualitatively the one it presupposes and from which it springs.[21]

The question now arises as to whether the definitive achievement of the necessary technological level, together with the "elimination of all additional repression", constitutes the necessary and sufficient condition for the development within "mature consciousness" of that *libidinous reason* by whose power "higher

[20] Marcuse is in entire agreement with Gehlen when it comes to the critical evaluation of this ethic of "moralized well-being": it hampers the main chances of human fulfilment. But in contrast with Gehlen he in no way puts the blame for this on the "subjectivity" which is the definitive starting-point of decay in collectively institutionalized and regulated morals. He blames rather the modern *"performance principle"* which has filled the vacuum of these traditionally grounded ethical systems: advanced as an end in itself, the principle is repressive, for it considers man as being in need, and as being open to programming. For him it is precisely and essentially the "conscious rational subject" led by a "new power of reason" that gives him hope for the possibility of a moral culture of "non-repressive sublimation" (*loc. cit.*, p. 196). Gehlen, on the other hand, with his Hobbesian ethic of the individual, only recognizes in the final analysis the alternative between "repressive sublimation" and "an ethic of tolerance which tends towards *laissez-faire* nihilism". This latter is the result of an "anthropological view of man as harmless" in which society becomes the "great warm culture-stall where the wild animals circle round each other, whispering ethical formulas" (A. Gehlen, "Der Pluralismus in der Ethik", in *Merkur*, 21, 1967, p. 117). Gehlen's latest work, recently published, *Moral und Hypermoral—eine pluralistische Ethik* (Frankfurt, 1969), only serves to confirm his position as described. The work appeared after the completion of this essay.

[21] Marcuse, *loc. cit.*, pp. 129 ff.

forms of cultural freedom" could really be achieved.[22] But pre-scinding entirely from that question for the time being, we can say that Marcuse is definitely right when he says of the collec-tively interpreted repressive ethics of order (in biblical language: the morals of Law) that they are solutions which must in the final analysis be "overpowered", for the sake of a really human fulfilment of man's existence. In this he is in basic agreement with Nietzsche and Hesnard.

Here, on the *secular* plane, albeit in an intellectual context which, from the anthropological point of view, is certainly still unsatisfactory, that central truth is touched upon which, from a theological point of view, seems in substance to have been dis-covered long ago. We need only look at the message of the New Testament. Neither *under* the "Law" nor *through* it does man attain to the full stature of which he is definitively capable as a moral being. In both Hesnard and Marcuse impulses are at work which in their moral core can certainly be connected with the ethos the New Testament reveals in its roughly outlined under-standing of human existence freed from repression: "There is no fear in love, but perfect love casts out fear."[23] We see this with Hesnard in his attempt to meet *right from the level of personal interaction* the *solipsistic* tendency of a repressive moral outlook which does nothing but frustrate itself away in guilt fears. He demands the "continual amelioration of interpersonal relations". And we see it with Marcuse when, with the same end in view (a moral outlook of "non-repressive sublimation"), he begins to ask about the possible socio-structural coefficients of such an out-look.

These attempts to solve the question are carried along by belief in the possibility of achieving a holier world. One can scarcely hold against them the very element which constitutes their speci-fic worth: that they try to approach this enormous problem from the *empirical* angle. Otherwise there would in fact be nothing left of them but an understanding of morals which could do no more than appeal to one's own sentiments in the matter. The decisive question is really, far more, whether ethical theories of this sort, conceiving of a world without guilt, can get any further

---

[22] *Ibid.*, pp. 196 f.   [23] 1 Jn. 4. 18.

than some sort of ideal utopia, without so twisting and turning in the process that they depart from that realm of reality which alone can liberate man to enjoy his own justice and truth.

II. Rehabilitating the Class-struggle

In view of the essential worldliness of the key in which man's life is written, any ethic committed to humanizing him must always, too, face up to the demands of conditioning his life in an empirical way; that means in a way that takes account of physiological, economic, psychological and socio-structural factors. These demands are still present even when one refuses to operate within the context of the "materialistic" fallacy that the moral essence of man, as the self-possessing person who comes into being through this humanizing process, is really no more than the sum of the factors which empirically condition him. If this last state of affairs were true, it would in fact seem possible to bring into existence the longed-for "moral society", the "kingdom of freedom and brotherhood", along purely empirical paths. But this idea is based on an illusion. In reality it is clear that the constituent essence of moral freedom does not *for one single moment* coincide *ontologically* with the factors which condition it, whatever form these may take and however positively they can be expressed; nor is it subject to any influence from them along the lines of natural causality. This is substantiated by the fact that man is capable of the highest moral activity even in the most difficult conditions: in conditions which are really quite inhuman when one looks at what fulfilled existence means. But it is substantiated equally well by the fundamental and enduring truth that there is no form of human endeavour whose whole being is not rooted in this freedom and sketched out in advance by it, whose whole ethical relevance and significance is not derived from it, and which can continue for a moment to exist as truly human, moral reality if the freedom on which it rests for its very possibility is taken to coincide with it or to exercise a causal influence on it. The ethical demand therefore remains that specifically empirical efforts be made to bring about the conditions for a "holy" world, a "healed" world; and it remains in spite of the insoluble dilemma posed by the basic structure of human moral existence, which sets *a priori* limits to all such efforts. The demand remains because the moral freedom, by whose power man *leads* his life, only finds the truly human presuppositions of its existence *in the moral and cultural developments formed from out of its own enduringly empirical substratum by these efforts.*

This basic anthropological analysis is also the foundation for all the ethical dignity there may be present in the *social struggle* that is being waged to make the world more human. This struggle is an eristic form of social interaction, imposing coercive restraints. But it does present us with an instrumental potency which has the advantage of generally leading to its goal with a speed and sureness that seems incomparably greater than anything one could conceive of in the case of a moral outlook of repression-free conviction. Nor is this all, for this instrumental potency is also able to raise up man's awareness of his own value without in the end destroying moral freedom again, in a way that is quite different from anything that could be achieved by an ethos of pure powerlessness. The genuine impulse of social criticism in such an ethos can only too easily be submerged in a "defeatist" moral attitude of renunciation, resignation to fate, and social subordination, in a way that serves only to confirm the prevailing injustice of society. And this is precisely because of its manifold "objective" incapacity.

It is only against this background that the enormous effect of Marxism can be understood: against the background of an ethic which in the name of love condemned the use of force, and which to all appearances was historically unsuccessful. Precisely through its condemnation of violence, and clean contrary to its original intentions, it became the aider and abettor of a moral submissiveness which, inverting its original inspiration, served only to petrify the existing power structure. Marxism is, from the political point of view, perhaps the most momentous social philosophy of modern times. It sets up a sort of rival model to what preceded it, when it makes the dialectic of class-warfare the cornerstone of all social progress.

The radically new element in this conception is undoubtedly the fact that the class-struggle is no longer considered an instrument by which power structures are just *changed round*; nor of

course is it considered to be a means for *preserving* the existing
structures; rather, it is essentially a factor helping towards the
birth of what is intended to be simply a *new order*, a *human*
ordering of all social relationships. According to Marx this will
reach its consummation in the appearance of the classless "communist" society, which will abolish all the inter-acting power
structures.

Marx's arguments for the legitimation of the class-struggle are
in their origins entirely from the field of moral anthropology.
This is clear above all in his critique of religion. He seeks to
establish from an anthropological starting-point the structures of
"alienation" in the historically determined individual, and first
and foremost here the religious factors which operate in these
structures. He starts from the concept of man as a radically self-
making being: "Man's roots are man himself."[24] And he goes
on to unfold out of this same critique the decisive axiological
conclusion that "man is, for man, the highest being".[25] In accordance with his genuine intention of criticizing structures, he then
goes on to draw this conclusion immediately out into the revolutionary imperative of "overthrowing every relationship in which
man finds himself degraded, enslaved, abandoned and despised
in his very being".[26]

This moral-anthropological approach to his proof does begin to
lose its relevance when Marx starts trying to see the practical
necessity of the revolutionary struggle as at the same time something necessitated by the very logic of history; something which,
with its consequent strict obedience to economic laws, guides the
whole process of man's social development. But it is consistent
with this notion, that the socio-economic milieu of wealth and
inhumanity deriving from the conditions of production and pro-
perty-control of those days should always be seen too as a milieu
of *class-struggle* that is specific to history. According to Marx this
milieu reaches its extreme point of growth in modern capitalism,
where it tends of necessity towards total revolutionary emancipation. And this emancipation, borne along on the shoulders of
the exploited class (which is itself a product of the capitalist

---

[24] K. Marx, "Contribution to the Critique of Hegel's Philosophy of
Right", in *Karl Marx, Early Writings*, ed. Bottomore (London, 1963).
[25] *Ibid.*   [26] *Ibid.*

system), effects the definitive abolition of private property. The higher form of society then comes necessarily into being.[27] Marx, then, believes that social development proceeds along a path that is known in advance, like a law of nature: the proletariat, the real executor of history's rationality, has the success of its enterprises guaranteed in advance. So it is entirely consistent of him to reject with horror all simple moral altruism; and to reject any social ethic which, though born of the will to reform society, aims at no more than a settlement of interests. For these activities only serve to delay what must and will, with historical necessity, come anyway.

The historico-logical objectivism which so characterizes Marxist social philosophy when it is developed "scientifically" as "historical materialism", constitutes in fact a social understanding of human activity that is in principle incapable of having any specifically *ethical* foundation. From this point of view Werner Sombart's interpretation is correct when he says "that 'there is not a single grain of ethics in the whole of Marxism, from one end to the other'; that theoretically Marx subordinates the 'ethical standpoint' to the 'principle of causality'; and that in practice this ethical standpoint looks only to the class-struggle".[28] This interpretation was later expressly confirmed and taken over by Lenin.

There is in fact a growing discrepancy between the doctrinaire prognoses of economic materialism and actual developments in the political, social and economic fields. And when it becomes apparent that no self-operative causal law of history does in fact exist, the "ethical standpoint" wins back all its very necessary significance. In the framework of real concrete history, progress

[27] Cf. here, *The Holy Family, or, Critique of Critical Critique* (Moscow, 1956).

[28] V. I. Lenin, "The Economic Content of Narodism and the criticism of it in Mr. Struve's Book", *Collected Works* (Moscow, 1963), vol. 1, pp. 337 ff. Accordingly, orthodox Marxism sees all ethics basically as a form of social consciousness determined, as is all consciousness, by "social existence", and so, finally, by prevailing economic relations. Cf. W. Eichhorn, *Wie ist Ethik als Wissenschaft möglich?* (Berlin, 1965): "From the Marxist point of view, ethics is the practical product and the lever of the process of history; it is a motive force ordered to the class-struggle and to the confrontation of different forms of society; a factor determined by the laws of history." *Ibid.*, p. 9.

has its roots far more in the creative potency of *man*, so it can only really take place in the measure that moral freedom is respected. For moral freedom is the cornerstone of human creativity, and so of all man's will to social progress. It is for this very reason, too, that the social struggle only shows up significantly on the page of human history when it has remained in fundamental subordination to the "ethical standpoint", refusing to follow the seductive glitter of a rationality which, in the name of utopian historical objectives, reduces man to the status of a tool. The same can be said of the widening of this social struggle, under the demands of *ultima ratio*, into a possible revolutionary struggle. E. Bernstein has already made the point against the orthodox Marxists that "the elevation of the material element into the omnipotent power of development" is a costly form of economic "self-deception", and that the belligerent drive for social progress therefore needs an ethical rather than a doctrinaire historical foundation.[29] This protest is in complete harmony with the ideas of those new exponents of Marxist revisionism who, like L. Kolakowski, assert that "the rules of moral conduct cannot be derived from any theory of historical progress"[30]—an assertion that is the result of immediate practical political experience of speculative historical objectivism working itself out in a thoroughly totalitarian manner. These writers see, rather, that historical progress itself must remain subject to the rules of moral conduct, and that in the long run progress has all its chances only when the means to it do not upset their end. For the Marxist Kolakowski this means that "not only Communism but also the movement towards it is a goal".[31] And this is no less than to say that the ethical goal stands already sketched out in the means to it; the fulfilment of the goal is morally inchoate in the path that leads towards it.

It is clear, then, that so far as Marxism is concerned the ethical

---

[29] E. Bernstein, *Evolutionary Socialism: a criticism and affirmation* (London, 1909). Cf. also H. Lübbe, *Politische Philosophie in Deutschland* (Basle, Stuttgart, 1963), pp. 117–25.

[30] L. Kolakowski, *Der Mensch ohne Alternative. Von der Möglichkeit und Unmöglichkeit Marxist zu sein* (Munich, 1967), p. 121.

[31] *Ibid.*, p. 213; and cf. here J. Habermas, "Zur philosophischen Diskussion um Marx und den Marxismus", in Habermas, *Theorie und Praxis* (Neuwied, Berlin, ²1967), pp. 261–355, esp. pp. 324 ff.

problem is essentially a problem about means. So when orthodox Marxism transposes all human praxis on to the historically objective level of the dialectical struggle, it comes out clearly as a system where the guilt factor is radically eliminated from this sphere of means. For within this dialectic man ceases in principle to be "an end in himself".[32] On the other hand the restoration of an ethical choice of means in the Revisionist position implies the restoration too of the possibility of guilt. Guilt always appears wherever man in the concrete is reduced in potency to the rank of a mere means. But it would be wrong to deduce from this that guilt-free activity means strife-free activity. For the impetus to engage in the class-struggle, rightly retained by the Revisionists from their Marxist inheritance, remains very much present as a positive motivated and motivating force of human and social self-realization, an inevitable factor in all historical progress.

Here another very basic dilemma comes to light. It concerns any activity dedicated to man and his humanization, and is found now in the field of the moral choice of means. For the medium of the class-struggle is only morally legitimate inasmuch as it is able to preserve for man his quality of being an "end in himself". And conversely, the medium of powerlessness can only remain ethical so long as it does not become identical with resignation, but continues to bear clear witness to the belligerent impulse towards the realization of a "holy world" even if for the sake of this holy world it must find its final consummation in the powerlessness of the Cross.

III. The Inauguration of Positive Reason

In so far as the Marxist critique of guilt concepts can still be

[32] According to Hermann Cohen, the "real founder of neo-Kantian socialism" (Lübbe, loc. cit., p. 109), all political achievement considered in its social dimension rests fundamentally on this Kantian development of the categorical imperative which sees "man as an end in himself, and thus differentiated from all that is 'merely a means'". For Cohen, Kant is therefore the "real, true creator of German socialism". (H. Cohen, "Einleitung mit kritischen Nachtrag", in F. A. Lange, Geschichte des Materialismus und Kritik seiner Bedeutung in der Gegenwart. Erstes Buch (Leipzig, [8]1908), pp. 524 f.—translated as The History of Materialism and criticism of its present importance (London, 1925).

said to operate on the level of *ethics*, it finally hits its target when it attacks that moral understanding within which the central impulse to engage in social struggle is discredited. It does not seem possible really to overcome social injustices if that impulse is not there. But with the growing importance of the empirical sciences another train of thought has arisen, bringing with it a critique of morality and guilt that is no less profound than the Marxist one. It is seen first of all as a method, but following the definite trend of Positivism it does flower into a systematic theory. It starts from the observation that the factors conditioning existence and the forms in which existence is fulfilled, whether outside man in Nature or proper to him alone, can all be reduced to a nexus of empirical laws and rules—to a nexus of determinable physiological, economic, psychological and socio-structural entities. This goes too for those factors we associate with moral value-judgments: with praise and blame, and with concepts of right and wrong, of good and of evil. In the measure that these complex correlations of conditions are unravelled by his reason, they become instruments at man's disposition, and the possibility arises of making human life "operable" and "manipulable" in the forms of its moral fulfilment. This is true even of the phenomenon of guilt; for guilt, being a *malum morale*, always implies in the first place a *malum*, and so presents itself as essentially not only a transcendental act of freedom grounded in the subject's deepest Self, but also a structural value that can be processed. And it follows that the actual concrete correlations of conditions operating in the intentional order can all, in every case, be grasped at the empirical level and so be neutralized in their effects.

There can be no doubt about the fact that the growth of the positive sciences, and the increasing refinement of methodological tools which goes with it, has opened up entirely new pathways into the structure of human existence. It has also opened up new and more effective ways of changing this structure, and of planning out more human structures for the future. All this is quite legitimate, too, in the light of current *theological* anthropology, which sees man as a being who, from the moment he first appeared on the plan of creation, has been given mastery over himself, and has been called to mould the reality around him in a human way—to impress on it the form of human sense. This process of moulding and informing reality has its own inherent rationality (*Rationalität*), of which it is an actualization, and which in an ever-increasing fashion lays bare the empirical factors that condition it, and disposes them to do their work. But it would be wrong simply to identify with this rationality the human power of reason (*Vernunft*) which determines the morality of the process and accepts responsibility for it. For the force of empirical rationality can work towards the realization of quite different ends. Growing insight into the structures of human existence and the laws by which it operates does bring with it the possibility of planning the future development of that existence; but it by no means creates of its own resources that power of reason which is able to judge and ratify the morality of the various formative processes which present themselves as possible.

The crucial failure of every positivist and neo-positivist theory of knowledge and metaphysics lies at this point. They see the essence of reason as lying simply in this methodological actualization of self-objectifying rationality; and consequently they see the way to a more human society and world as the way of positive reason itself. This is clear, for example, in the evolutionary conceptions and social theories of such varied thinkers as Popper,[33] Huxley,[34] Fourastié,[35] Geiger[36] and Albert.[37] These theories continue a tradition whose origins can be found as far back as Laplace,[38] and which was promoted especially by Quetelet and Le

[33] K. R. Popper, *The Open Society and its Enemies*, 2 vols. (London, 1950).

[34] J. Huxley, *Essays of a Humanist* (London, 1964); also *Evolution, the Modern Synthesis* (London, 1942).

[35] J. Fourastié, *Le grand espoir du 20me siècle* (Paris, 1949).

[36] Th. Geiger, *Arbeiten zur Soziologie.—Methode, Moderne Grossgesellschaft, Rechtssoziologie, Ideologiekritik* (Berlin, 1962); also *Vorstudien zu einer Soziologie des Rechts* (Neuwied, Berlin, 1964).

[37] H. Albert, *Traktat über kritische Vernunft* (Tübingen, 1968). For a critique of Albert and Popper cf. esp. J. Habermas, *Theorie und Praxis* (Neuwied, Berlin, ²1967), pp. 251 ff.; also his "Analytische Wissenschaftstheorie und Dialektik", in *Logik der Sozialwissenschaften*, ed. E. Topitsch (Cologne, Berlin, ²1965), pp. 291 ff.

[38] It was Laplace who in his *Théorie analytique des probabilités* (Paris, 1812) made the first attempts to develop probability calculation as a method applicable to the "moral sciences" and to social realities.

Play.[39] It is a tradition guided in particular by the methodological aim of applying the rational procedures of natural science in the field of the "moral sciences", and of subjecting to mathematical calculation the socio-cultural process of forming human reality. It received its most forceful and systematic expression, perhaps, in the work of Cournot, for whom human history is essentially the history of a continual rational penetration and planning of the factors which morally condition man, and one that reaches its final consummation and vanishing-point in the *posthistoire* of a totally rationalized self-administering world.[40] This world of *posthistoire* is, according to Cournot, not carried along by any new faith, nor any new meaning, nor any new ethos, but only by that rationality which penetrates its every limb and leads it to its necessary fulfilment. *"Humanité sans âme"* is what Ruyer called the rule of this sort of reason.[41]

In opposition to all this it must be made quite clear that all those factors that, thanks to this rationality, can be counted, reckoned, planned and altered, are not in their turn merely measurable entities; they are, rather, composed in their very essence of elements in the intentional order which are determined by ethos and built up into meaningful structures of human interests and values. These structures are themselves the product of a power of reason grounded in the transcendental freedom which grows in the heart of man's relation to himself—a freedom elevated beyond all question of subordination (*Verfügbarkeit*), for it is itself the ordaining principle (*Verfügende*) in the world. It becomes evident here, therefore, that all plan-forming rationality which aims to change the *conditio humana* lives basically from the truth that the object of its ordinations is itself a subject, and must remain so if the plan is ever to achieve reality. Man is in his deepest Self a subject, and is so inalienably. It is not a question of what he ought to be, but of what he is; for socio-cultural processes are

[39] A. Quetelet, *Essai sur l'homme et le développement de ses facultés ou Essai de physique sociale*, 2 vols. (Paris, 1835); F. Le Play, *Les ouvriers européens, études sur les travaux, la vie domestique et la condition morales des populations ouvrières de l'Europe, précédées d'un exposé de la méthode d'observation* (Paris, 1855).

[40] A. A. Cournot, *Considerations sur la marche des idées et les événements dans les tempts modernes*, 2 vols. (Paris, 1872).

[41] P. Ruyer, *L'Humanité de l'avenir d'après Cournot* (Paris, 1930), p. 97.

founded on persons: on beings, therefore, that are capable of insight and assent. Consequently any attempt to control society that aimed to reduce man to the level of radical subordination proper to an unreasoning object which could react only with the reflexes of Nature, would end up by abolishing the very preconditions of its own existence: beings that do not understand are *socially* uncontrollable.

This does not mean of course that techniques of mastery over Nature cannot be applied in the field of social control. For in the very framework of these ontologically rooted conditioning factors about which we have spoken, a wide field of play opens out for the manipulation of man. The social engineer can evaluate man in his bare and basic power to give assent; and he can programme him by social, psychological and possibly even biogenetic processes to follow a plan he, the engineer, has made. And these processes leave the individual no chance any more to examine the plan by the criteria of moral truth and reason, so that he might assume responsibility for it. It follows that this sort of social praxis here termed *socio-cybernetic*—has its necessary correlative in a functional understanding of human activity which equates morality (as that permanently "personal" dimension of the control process) with the will to implement the plan and readiness to adapt to it, and which consequently has to interpret guilt with equal rigour as refusal to function (*Dysfunktionalität*) and so as unadaptedness to the plan.

Contrasting with this is another sort of social control-praxis— one to which alone the term *social cybernetics* should be applied.[42] It uses these same rational, socio-technological procedures, but does so in such a way that the critical powers of the object under control remain fundamentally involved in the controlling plan, which therefore undergoes a permanent transformation. These control-systems are essentially co-ordinations of *subjects* who have dealings with each other and exercise influence on each other; and they are essentially open to development. So they imply an ethic which sanctions not only obedience to the plan in its normative demands, but also responsibility for the reasonableness and truth of the plan itself. And it necessarily follows that within

[42] And cf. here W. Korff, "Empirical Social Study and Ethics", in *Concilium*, 5, 4 (1968), pp. 9–11 (American edn., vol. 35).

the framework of these systems the factor of conflict and refusal to function has a positive and constructive meaning. Only a control-system that allows contradiction stands any chance of ever evolving to its climax in a "better world." In such a system, the normative critical reasoning power of the individual is linked in a permanent intentional process to the normative reason inherent in the control-plan itself.

Both of these control-systems are possible. And inherent in each of them is an inescapable moral dimension, for they are both social systems. When we take this moral dimension as a criterion by which to compare them, we see that the socio-cybernetic system understands evil (considered as *malum morale*) as realizing itself in the form of insubordination by the individual towards the system; the social cybernetic system on the other hand sees it as lying in a lack of critical awareness. This lack takes the shape in the individual of conformity to the system, and in the system itself it takes the shape of an authoritarian and repressive structure which refuses to be scrutinized critically by the individual's power of reason. But whatever different emphasis and interpretation these two systems may give to *malum morale*, in this they agree, that they are themselves no more than specific attempts to employ certain rational empirical procedures with a view to overcoming the deep-seated milieu of crisis in which man's experience of his existence takes place. By means of these procedures they aim to do away with this crisis-milieu in its structure of *malum*, and so to abolish the evil that is in the world. Both socio-cybernetics and social cybernetics, then, tend towards the realization of a "guilt-free ethic", understood in a purely secular way. And it is precisely there that the deep dilemma of each system lies. For the question about the ultimate reasonableness of any planning cannot be answered from within the system itself, without the danger of either ending up in a socio-cybernetically organized and managed world from which the historical element has been banished as meaningless, or of ending up in the liberalizing aimlessness of a nihilistic, social cybernetic system of *laissez-faire*. The different attempts to solve the problem align themselves in different ways, but none of these alignments can be evaluated positively and decisively by appealing to any immanent logic and reasonableness.

This final and positive evaluation, with its power to give an ultimate lead and inspiration to all man's knowledge and dealings, and to bring on the crisis immanent in his milieu in the world by putting order and direction into the rational attempts to solve it, exists in God's definitive word of acceptance to his work. It exists in God's "Yes", grounded in his act of creation, sealed and ratified in Christ's act of salvation; in the "Yes" that bears the burden of all being, persevering through all its falls and guilt, conserving and redeeming the meaning of each individual and the meaning of the whole. Man accepts this "Yes" of God, and takes it into himself in faith; and in the world it assumes concrete existence in the faith man has in man. It thus becomes in turn the ultimate ethical criterion of all man's activity: a criterion by which all submissiveness and all criticism, all law and all freedom, all strife and all love, all moral and all technological procedures of human planning and control can and must be measured. Man's belief in man lives from God's redeeming "Yes"; and by its light the truth of guilt and evil can be seen to lie finally in the mystery of self-rejection and un-faith. By its light too, every attempt to eradicate the world's milieu of crisis solely by the strength of the freedom-seeking reason that lies in the world, can be seen to be a *petitio principii*.

Translated by J. T. Swann

Jacques-Marie Pohier

The Hermeneutic of Sin in the Light of Science, Technology and Ethics

"IN a world governed by science and technology how can the term moral evil be used in theology and preaching?" Stated in these terms the question assigned to this article by the editors of this number of *Concilium* is relevant perhaps only to a limited part of the Christian world. For example, it is irrelevant to the Church in Africa, Asia or South America. Despite the universal nature of revelation it is difficult to claim in this case that it is of world-wide application if we take into account the great differences in experiences and cultures. But within these limits, not always easy to discern or to bypass, the question is relevant for theology and catechesis in their proclamation of what revelation has to say about sin to men of our scientific and technological civilization. But the actual fact of this difficulty may seem something of a paradox.

I. SCIENCE, TECHNOLOGY AND ETHICS IN THE FACE OF MORAL EVIL

As a matter of fact it could be said that theologians and preachers are almost alone in such a world in being unable to talk of moral evil. Each of the various disciplines, technological processes and ideologies which shape this scientific and technological world speaks of something which certainly comes under what we call moral evil; they interpret it and suggest means to combat it. Marxism, for example, which claims to be the result of a scientific analysis of economic and socio-political phenomena, develops a real morality: the class struggle, the alienation of work and concepts like those of deviationism or revisionism possess an interpretative value in this context: they result in a process whose object is to combat all these forms of evil. The various psychological and pedagogical disciplines by their insistence on the development and structurization, or the loss of function and structure, of the different psychical functions or of the personality, contribute greatly to the way in which man can harm himself or others. These disciplines also formulate concepts which possess an interpretative value in this context: lack of adjustment, regression, immaturity, and so on. And even if they hardly appeal to the category of moral responsibility, they result in human beings, either individually or collectively, regulating their own behaviour. Psychoanalysis, for its part, has perceived the importance of guilt, aggression, hate, and so on. Here again the interpretation and theory lead to a course of action to which it would be wrong to assign ethical aims (or even exclusively therapeutic ones), but as the work of Freud himself shows, it has a practical relevance for individuals as for cultures.

Examples could be multiplied: the economic, demographic and sociological sciences or techniques, even the biological and natural sciences, have an enormous moral incidence. Modern Western culture therefore finds no difficulty in speaking of the evil of man or of the evil that man does; it frequently offers interpretations and almost always means of combating it.

It may seem surprising, therefore, that theologians, priests and believers are unable to win a hearing when they want to pass on what Revelation has to say about the evil of man and the evil that man does. Yet our pastoral methods and theology know well that their message is not heard; men of our times assert that this message is almost meaningless to them, and that it is even plain contrary to their own experience of evil and the interpretation which they try to give to it. But surprise at this can hardly continue when it is seen that in the different disciplines mentioned above there is certainly a question of evil and perhaps of morality, but there is probably no question of moral evil and certainly not of sin.

It may seem paradoxical that there can be a question of evil and of morality but not of moral evil, when we are obviously not referring to physical evil. But since Kant a clear-cut separation

has been effected between morality and ethics the consequences
of which are conclusive for our subject. Hegel formulated this
separation, which is fully accepted by contemporary culture as
a whole, characterizing the passing from morality to ethics as
the passage from the concrete but subjective realization of freedom to the concrete and objective realization of freedom in history. Of course, in both cases it will always be a question of doing
good and avoiding evil; but avoiding evil or doing it do not mean
the same thing in both cases. For the subjective realization of
freedom it will be enough to live the virtuous life as it was understood by Plato and Aristotle or in obedience to the law as
understood by the Stoics and after them by the long tradition of
Christian morality. This is by no means enough for the objective
realization of freedom by which ethics is now defined. It is not
that ethics despises virtue or the law, but because it requires more,
and in any case something else: the concrete realization of freedom in the objectivity of the world. To do good does not mean
so much what Aristotle said of it, that virtue is what makes man
good and makes his work good; it has a far more objective meaning: to be good means realizing freedom in the objects of the
world. To do evil is not so much to do what makes man bad and
makes his work bad, but it means evasion of, or failure to
achieve, this realization. The difference is such that precisely
those two expressions, "moral good" and "moral evil", have
practically disappeared from the vocabulary of ethics. This is not
the sign of a-morality, but shows that there is something different
at stake.

Now the various undertakings which characterize our modern
Western world are derived from the same culture and the same
state of mind as is evidenced by these philosophies—science and
technology are a realization of man in the objectivity of the
world. This is true of the natural sciences. It is still truer of the
human sciences—sociology, economics, politics, psychology, lin-
guistics, and so on deal with the most typical media for the
realization of freedom in the objectivity of the world: work,
money, politics, culture, language, and so on. It is normal, therefore, for these sciences and techniques to be full of the ethical
concerns and extensions mentioned above, but for their ethical
meaning to be difficult of formulation in terms of moral good

and moral evil in the sense implied by pre-Kantian and pre-Hegelian moral theory.

II. SCIENCE, TECHNOLOGY AND ETHICS IN THE FACE OF CHRISTIAN EXPERIENCE OF SIN

If it is not a question of moral evil in the classical sense of the term, still less is it one of sin in the Christian meaning. As the Bible and Tradition both lay down, sin is a breach with God leading to a separation from God. This breach and this separation, brought about by man, derive their whole meaning from the prior and prevenient act of God when he made the covenant with man and proposed that he should live by and with him. Sin therefore can have no meaning for one who has no idea of the existence of a personal God, *a fortiori* for one who does not believe that God makes a covenant with man, that this act on God's part is the most important event in the history of a man and of humanity, and that the reference of human action and human existence to this covenant becomes the most important reference of all those which endow man's acts and existence with their true significance. Now the experience of reality from which modern science and technology derive and which they systematize is not open to these different convictions which form the necessary preliminaries to a sense of sin. Indeed this experience is of a kind which causes these ideas, and consequently sin itself, to seem unmeaningful and indeed non-sense.

For example, knowledge of the physical universe does not allow the natural sciences to understand this world as the creation of God; nor do the theory of relativity, the various hypotheses on the origin of the world, the theory of evolution, the laws of genetics and physiology have any need to introduce the Creator-God as a factor in the explanation of the phenomena of nature; the explanation of these phenomena which they provide is self-sufficient within the epistemological boundaries of these sciences. And the various technical processes arising from these sciences have no need to posit the intervention of God's original and continuing creative act, or his providential action, as one of the factors at work in the systematization of nature and its management. Their own working tools suffice. In consequence, not only is the

"God-Factor" useless, but more especially it loses any possibility of having a meaning, for any action that he might have would on this view belong to an order different from that of those factors experienced and discussed by science and technology; it is entirely alien to them.

In more recent times the emergence of the human sciences has had consequences that have been less clearly discerned. None the less, they are of crucial importance for the subject concerning us, for in this case man's existence and actions are concerned. Man's most characteristic qualities and activities such as knowledge, language, love, culture, history, political and economic reality and even religion are now the object of scientific investigation. And this investigation has no more need of bringing in God as an explanatory factor than have the natural sciences. Similarly, technical processes deriving from the human sciences no more need to introduce the "God-Factor" in their systematization and treatment of the phenomena in question than do the technical processes in the natural sciences. Here again, not only is the "God-Factor" useless, but it loses any possibility of being meaningful; once more God becomes something alien.

In addition, even if the human and natural sciences make no claim to understand, explain or accomplish everything, what lies beyond their knowledge or capacity does not seem to them a space left empty in which God could fit into the scheme. It appears merely as the space at present out of their reach which one day they will obtain or, more radically still, as the sign of human limitation, but a limitation all the same which does not refer them to God. God is alien even to the experience that science and technology have of their own limitations.

This represents an extraordinary cultural revolution whose consequences our modern world seems scarcely to have perceived. Believers probably are more clearly aware of them than most people: it is enough for them to look back on their own tradition to perceive the position occupied by the "God-Factor" in the understanding of the world and of man, and how far experience of the world and of man formed, in this tradition, the living springs of the experience of God.

To this must be added an observation which gives direction to the rest of my remarks, for it is of capital importance in understanding the faith in the context of the modern world. Until the advent of the sciences and technological methods just mentioned it was possible for believers to think through their experience of man and the world on the one hand, and their experience of God revealing himself and making a covenant, on the other, in the same set of categories, precisely because of the place occupied by God in their understanding of the world and of man. Creation and covenant, Providence and salvation, nature and supernature, man's natural life and his divine life, theodicy and theology, could be dovetailed into a synthesis of thought.

This it seems to me explains, at least in part, the trend of the past ten years or so in the interpretation of the faith and more especially of sin. For it is quite obvious that if sin is meaningless save as a break with God and the frustration of the covenant, it can scarcely have any meaning for the modern culture described above. Of course this does not mean that this culture does not face the question of man's evil and the evil that he does; I have emphasized this point already. But to interpret this evil in relation to God and a covenant with God is completely foreign to it; here again, on the contrary, it is this interpretation which would alienate it from its own experience of evil.

III. THEOLOGICAL AND PASTORAL REACTIONS

How did theology, and pastoral practice, react to what seems indeed to be a complete deadlock in any possible interpretation of sin?

The most concerted reaction on the part of believers has been to adopt this "foreignness" of God and take it to its logical conclusion. Of course, God is quite other; of course, his word and his covenant come to us from elsewhere and not from our world; neither God nor the life that he originated in man forms part of the objectivity of the world. The essential content of God's revelation cannot be understood by man through investigation of his own world and his human state. And this is so even if by the use of analogy he pursues his investigation as far as the God who is thought to be at the origin of this world and this state. In the same way, the Christian mystery of sin is not to be deduced by

man from the evil in the world and his human state. In relation
to the psychological, sociological or moral experiences of guilt,
transgression of the law and the failure of morality, in relation
also to the evil in the world and the evil which arises from the
world, sin also is something quite "other". Here we can see some
of the most fruitful fields of inquiry in modern theology with its
insistence on the originality, the otherness, the brutality, even, of
the invasion of the gospel message.

But perhaps it has not been sufficiently observed that by the
same token the separation between the word of God and the
objectivity of the world was ratified, even to the extent of seeing
this separation as one of the Gospel's distinctive marks. For against
the objectivity of the world, in the name of the Gospel it could
be urged, "the word judges the world". And just as the revelation of the word could have for its mission denunciation of the
claims of freedom and its realization in the objectivity of the
world, in the same way revelation concerning sin could (or must)
be the criterion for judging guilt and the law. Not only does sin
stand revealed as "other" but it forms the touchstone, or rather
the stumbling-block, for ethics as well as for morality antecedent
to ethics. In the last resort a genuinely Christian idea of sin, it
would seem, can only be constructed on the ruins of morality
and ethics, and will itself have to undertake this task of destruction.

This reaction, moreover, can find support in the varying ideas
in modern philosophy and culture. Directly Hegel had confirmed
the transition from morality to ethics and had defined the latter's
task by the realization of freedom in the objectivity of the world,
Kierkegaard adopted the role of prophet of the transition beyond
ethics and denounced it as real alienation. The sequel in modern
philosophical development shows that his protest should be taken
seriously. But religious thought, without always being fully aware
of the difficulty of the problem, was to plunge into this breach
effected in the objectivity of the world and to believe that the use
of this kind of language enabled it both to counter the imperious
relationship of freedom and the world to talk about God in a
way no longer entirely alien to modern culture.

On the other hand, both scientific and technological thought,
and generally speaking the realization of freedom in the

objectivity of the world, experienced its own ups and downs. The whole complex of close relationships that it was desired to establish between man and the world proved to be harsh or ineffective, either injuring man or leaving large gaps. Its protagonists were not the last to be aware of the limitations of the undertaking, which is all the more significant since they nevertheless continued to pursue it with some success. But it was logical that coupled with this awareness came a challenge to the undertaking, taking many violent forms, as is well known today. Equally naturally, people sought to fill in the big gaps. So in our present world trends can be observed endeavouring to fill this vacant space with something beyond ethics, beyond science and technology, at any rate with an "aside". The vogue for imaginative realism (le réalisme fantastique) started by the Planète movement in France is a good example. Here again religious thought attempted to discover a favourable opening for a language about God and for an awakening of man's religious mind. This despite the fact that it led straight to the "stop-gap God" for which classical apologetics was severely criticized. Once again we find confirmation of the fact that God's place is necessarily to be found in the void left by the whole scheme of ethics, science and technology.

Despite their great differences, not only of inspiration but also of religious and human quality, these various reactions therefore have this in common: they confirm the radical opposition between the sphere revealed by the word of God and that wherein freedom in the objectivity of the world is realized. Almost all our theology and pastoral practice in regard to sin and to the whole Christian mystery subsist on this opposition. For it is not enough to add on afterwards what is called "horizontalism" as a correction to any excess in the "verticalism" of a certain idea of the word of God. Both horizontalism and verticalism, since they originate from premises of this kind, are doomed to be two disjunctive dimensions incapable of constituting a genuine sphere. As regards sin this disjunction finds expression in the radically heterogeneous nature of sin as a breaking of the covenant and rejection of the word of God in connection with the various experiences which man has of evil—experiences originating in relation to himself, to others and to his world.

Now these tendencies in theology and pastoral practice seem

to me to bring our understanding of the faith to a deadlock. Obviously I do not mean to reject their usefulness nor to deny that they do justice to certain fundamental aspects of Revelation and Tradition. But it does appear difficult to follow them to their logical conclusions, particularly in the form popularized by the theology and pastoral methods now current. The deadlock to which they lead appears clearly from an examination of what Revelation has to say about sin, even if this is confined to the vocabulary of the Bible alone. In the Hebrew Old Testament there are no less than fifty terms to designate what we mean by the one word "sin". And the Greek New Testament makes use of derivatives from five roots. But, more especially, each of these words is far from possessing only one meaning and the inter-changes are numerous and complex. Of course, the sense of break with God, rejection of the word and the covenant, be-comes increasingly the principal meaning, but never in such a way as to rule out other dimensions of sin like transgression of the law, the disorder brought into society, in man and even in the world, the stain that it imparts, guilt, and so on. In the Bible sin does not have a single meaning; rather is it an analogical reality not only in the sense understood by St Thomas in con-nection with the distinctions between mortal and venial sin or original and actual sin, but by the plurality of its dimensions.

By the reduction of this diversity to a single meaning, even to the most specific of them all, the word's many senses and applica-tions in the Bible are left out of account. On the other hand there is a danger of destroying the harmony of God's creative and saving plan for man, since a reduction of this kind is a neglect of realities which, also by the action of God, form constituent dimensions of the human state. Such are, society, law, order and disorder in the world and, even on a last analysis, guilt. Now it is no function of the advent of the gospel message to separate man from these different realities nor, in consequence, to separate sin from these various points of reference.

IV. PROLEGOMENA TO A HERMENEUTIC OF SIN

Theology and pastoral practice might well have avoided the excessive nature of this *ad unum* if they had taken more seriously

the nature of the scientific, technological and ethical developments as defined above. There is no need to remain enclosed
within the confines of these developments. There is something
beyond ethics, science and technology. I do not claim that it
would be enough to take these developments seriously to be able
to work out a hermeneutic which would make the truth of
Christian teaching on sin obvious, for this teaching, like that of
the covenant, is definitely one of Death and Resurrection, folly
and a scandal. But it seems to me that Christian thought so far
has not taken seriously enough the characteristic values of the
scientifico-technological and ethical development. It has been far
too eager, on the excuse that they actively call for something
further, to desire to transcend them. Now here as in every other
field, before transcending it is necessary to "catch up". And also
to pass through, to remain there, for this transcendence will
never be anything but a dialectical phenomenon in which what
is transcended forms an integral part. So long as Christian
thought has not effected this passing through or made this
sojourn it has no chance of being able to understand and formulate its faith in a way that will make it intelligible to contemporary culture.

In doing this it could encounter values which could contribute
to a renewed understanding of its mysteries and would enable it
to show certain aspects more clearly than it could on the basis of
other values (which none the less are by no means superseded).
The realization of freedom in the history and objectivity of the
world might well prove to be a theme that could promote a certain interpretation of God's plan in creation as well as in salvation. It would of course concern the freedom of God and it is
in this sense that the Christian message remains a folly and a
scandal. But at least this folly and this scandal would be given
expression in a problem which is that of contemporary culture
and which seems as much in keeping with it as the classical
ontological problem. Possibly it would be even better fitted to
bring out clearly, on the subject of creation and salvation, how
God's action is really historical and constitutive of the objectivity of the world, and how man's vocation is to realize his
own effective freedom in connection with the realization of God's
freedom itself. Concerning sin, such an idea of the action of God

and the action of man would perhaps enable the separation already mentioned to be overcome, the breaking of the covenant retaining its originality and pre-eminence. All the same it will not seem to belong to an order so radically foreign to a man's experience of the evil of which he is the source.

Now this experience also includes values which could help towards a better understanding of sin, values which, it must be said, this better understanding must make its own. Actually when it is a case of authentic human values and it is asserted in addition that man is made in the image of God, it is impossible to separate the realization by man of his freedom in these genuine human activities and the realization of God's plan which the freedom of God has entrusted to the freedom of man. The experience of law, for example, is an important human experience. And something essential for man is at work in political, social, economic, juridical activity and so on. Now the idea and reality of law, the relationship of man with the law, its establishment, its efficacy, but also the breaking of the law possess in all these activities a fundamental value. In the same way the relationship of man with the world, its ordering or disorganization by man, forms a decisive experience inherent in man's history, since to be guilty belongs perhaps to the fact that he is man, and is therefore contingent in the order of good and evil as in every other order. If in the realization of his freedom these experiences act as the constitutive factors which the scientifico-technological and ethical scheme of things acknowledges them to be, religious thought must refuse radically to separate the order of these experiences from that of experience of sin.

This refusal, rather, must be made not in the name of a system of human values, perfectly legitimate though it may be, but in the name of faith. For on the one hand it believes that man is the image of God: and so it is in some sort the very freedom of God that man realizes when he begins the task of realizing his own freedom by the ways proper to his own state; the evil that his freedom then causes is indeed an evil before God, an evil in relation to God, and so a sin. On the other hand, faith believes that God made his covenant with man; its God is a God present among us. However profound the transformation to which man is called, and to which he is raised by this covenant, it does not make him anything else than a man, even if it does make him a son of God. The covenant does not enable man to escape creation nor does the experience of sin save him from the experience of evil. And that is the reason that Revelation and Tradition have never scrupled to show transgression of the law, the breakdown of worldly structures and guilt as the particular factors in terms of which the relationship of man with the God of the covenant and the mystery of its breaking by man through sin had to be lived and understood.

If religious thought at the present time is reluctant to do the same, actually it is because these different realities now have a very different meaning from that which they possessed in previous cultures; their "interpretation", like that of sin, must therefore be different. Because it seems clear that the old interpretations no longer fully make sense, and it does not yet appear what form the new ones could take, it is thought better to keep silence, or that it is enough to mention the old ones merely to expose their shortcomings. But if the meaning of these experiences has changed, their primary importance in relation to man has only been given greater emphasis; their disappearance or elimination from the theological and pastoral formulation of sin is no guarantee, therefore, of the authenticity of the Christian understanding of sin, but rather the opposite.

The way seems open therefore for a hermeneutic of sin aimed at a world governed by the scientifico-technological and ethical scheme of things characteristic of our Western world today. After all, this culture does not lack experiences of evil and these experiences are far from being alien to revelation on sin. But religious thought has not yet taken this path—this task is still before it and not behind it. For it to start on this way, it seems to me, there is one essential condition. It is that only those believers, whether they be priests or laity, theologians, pastors or representatives of the magisterium, who are fully involved in the scientifico-technological undertaking, that is, only those who genuinely belong to our modern Western culture, can bring such an enterprise to a successful conclusion. Religious people wonder how to formulate a hermeneutic of sin for man involved in, or produced by this scheme of things. But this man remains alien to religion; he comes face to face with it because it is outside him.

It speaks to him in the way missionaries might speak to people whose culture they do not share. The question discussed in this article can never be answered—how, that is, approach the men of this scientifico-technological world to speak to them of sin—so long as it is not changed into another question, the one men ask themselves when they wish to hear the message of revelation on sin to formulate it for themselves and for those like them. Then, and only then, can such a hermeneutic of sin be established.

Translated by Lancelot Sheppard

PART II
BULLETIN

Werner Post

The Problem of Evil

THE continuing failure to explain the nature of evil appears to have driven modern researchers to restrict their inquiries to individual disciplines. Wise or legitimate, it is a change that could well achieve at least partial success. But for philosophy, and particularly for theology, the reality of evil will nevertheless remain a central concern. The objection that one should not speak of things that one cannot demonstrate merely places the question of evil on a level with insoluble mathematical problems. To say nothing about evil would be tantamount to declaring that it was inescapable destiny.

Voltaire argued that any attempt to explain evil by recourse to the Deity was suspect. It would be better "not to believe in a God at all than to reproach him for something that man is punished for. ... That [theory] would identify God with evil itself, immeasurable and purposeless, which has created sentient beings for no other object than to make them eternally miserable; or it would make out that God is the personification of powerlessness and imbecility, capable neither of foreseeing nor preventing the misery of his creation."[1] Though there is much one could say about Voltaire's position on the subject of evil, that is not my intention. What is under discussion in this article is *malum morale*, not *malum physicum*, or theodicy.

Given the enormous injuries mankind has inflicted on itself,

[1] Voltaire, *Dictionnaire philosophique portatif* (1794); English translation *Philosophical Dictionary*, selected and translated by H. I. Woolf (London, 1923).

Voltaire's sharply expressed disdain for Leibniz's theodicy appears to be comparable to the neo-scholastic acquiescence in a classification of the different levels of evil and in the old argument that it is so much better for man to be left free to recognize God, and that on these terms God is willing to allow the possibility of evil.[2]

Of a quite different and much more serious nature is the interest shown in the problem of evil from the more recent ontological viewpoint.[3] Here, evil is seen not as a mere absence of good or weakness of will, but as "negation of the good becoming conscious of itself". This remains paradoxical in as far as the denial of good in turn intends something good; it is a case of good in conflict with what is good in the will. The will is ".... its own operative source, the centre from which its own being is decided and with it, in consenting and formative activity, everything else, the world as a whole".[4] Being, the self-communicating origin, comes first; dependent on it, the will and the perceived good accord, and a decision follows. Evil, therefore, can only be a discordance of good within the will; if the good is the harmonious order of the whole, then "evil is the discord of a being with itself".[5] The enabling cause of evil rests within the will itself because the will is finite: as finite *will* it is good, as *finite* will it is in discord with its origin and so must first always recover itself. This internal conflict, "the being of finite mind, is the ground of the possibility of evil".[6]

In this context, any thought of being able to dispose of evil must sound absurd, for it would amount to the quite meaningless attempt to resolve the essential and prior tension between being and existent, existence and essence. This is the will's situation, it has to "be alive to" the "origin", the "centre", and accord with it.

But this approach to our subject is in part tautological as the will cannot perceive anything other than itself; its own transcendental extension into the infinite turns out to be that centre and

---

[2] *Philosophisches Wörterbuch*, ed. W. Brugger (Freiburg, [7]1959), p. 41.
[3] G. Siewerth, *Die Freiheit und das Gute* (Freiburg, 1959); B. Welte, *Über das Böse* (Freiburg, 1959); K. Hemmerle, "Evil", in *Sacramentum Mundi*, II (London and New York, 1968), pp. 279–83.
[4] Hemmerle, *art. cit.*, p. 281.   [5] Hemmerle, *art. cit.*, p. 282.
[6] Hemmerle, *art. cit.*, p. 282.

origin which the same will must attune itself to. Averting evil means concern for what is good, an action that rests on criteria that cannot be ontologically demonstrated.

This concludes the philosophical argumentation and is the point at which it merges appropriately into the theological.

This objection has also been raised against Kant's doctrine of radical evil. Goethe maintained that Kant had indulged in philosophical rhetoric for the sake of gaining ground among Christians.[7] Karl Barth sees elements of Christian soteriology appearing unexpectedly "like incongruous guests".[8] The liberal side of Kantian research has designated Kant's *Religion within the Limits of Reason Alone* (1793) as "compromise", as "the not readily enjoyable fruit of pure criticism".[9]

Kant's theory, challenged by the freedmen of the Enlightenment as well as by the slaves of orthodoxy, departs radically from Rousseau's gospel of nature or Leibniz's metaphysics of pre-established harmony. In what follows, my comments will be restricted to those arising from Kant's essay: the theodicy problem,[10] and related aspects of philosophy of religion, will not be considered.

According to Kant, a man is morally evil "not because what he does is evil (against the law), but because what he does is such as to inculcate in him evil maxims".[11] Thus, evil is not an empirical fact but an evil maxim that derives from it and that ultimately negates moral law. Weakness of will, instinct-determined actions —in fact, empirical causes generally—cannot give rise to evil maxims; the cause here is rather a propensity in man that

[7] Goethe to Herder, Letter of 7.6.1793.

[8] Karl Barth, *Die Protestantische Theologie im 19. Jahrhundert* (Zollikon-Zürich, ²1952), pp. 257–72.

[9] H. Glockner, *Hegel*, I (Stuttgart, 1929), p. 245; he calls Kant's book "a dead book" (p. 247). Similar comments are to be found in Troeltsch and Cassirer.

[10] Cf. on the theodicy problem in Kant, W. Oelmüller, *Die unbefriedigte Aufklärung* (Frankfurt, 1969); also a detailed discussion of the theodicy question and a rigorous critique of Kant's philosophy of religion (cf. especially pp. 159–88, 218–38).

[11] I. Kant, *Die Religion innerhalb der Grenzen der blossen Vernunft*; English translation *Religion within the Limits of Reason Alone* (Glasgow, 1934).

freedom does not preclude, even when evil is inherent in it; for if man were evil by nature, responsibility could not be imputed to him. Kant therefore diagnoses in man, in addition to the general infirmity of his nature and the self-interestedness of his moral principles, a "corrupt heart" and a "propensity towards arbitrariness within ethical maxims, a tendency to belittle moral law principles in favour of others (i.e., immoral ones)".[12]

To describe man as *evil* is to say that although he is aware of the moral law, he has permitted deviations from it to enter into his ethical maxims. To describe him as evil *by nature* is to make a statement about the human species as such, without, however, affirming that as such it cannot act other than evilly; rather is one presupposing in any man, including the best of men, a "subjectively necessary" propensity towards evil. Freedom and universality, Kant observes, will not willingly be harnessed; ultimately, however, "we shall have to call this natural tendency towards evil, and the tendency itself—because it is always a self-incurred fault—a radical and inherent (but none the less culpable for that) evil in human nature".[13] Its radicalness, by which is meant its deep-rooted position in human nature, Kant considers evident, as can most clearly be seen, he himself points out, in the case of primitive peoples.

As this line of argumentation does nothing to resolve the tension between freedom and evil, critics have always latched on to alleged theological prejudices in Kant.[14] They point out that even if the tendency towards evil is inherent, it would not find actual expression unless man set evil ethical maxims above good ones. Neither the sense faculties nor reason evilly inclined can cause evil; the cause must be sought in conation; in other words, it must be attributed to the sphere of morals; "this evil is radical evil because it corrupts the ground of all maxims".[15]

Unlike the biblical theories of original sin, Kant cannot agree

---

[12] *Loc. cit.*, p. 677 (Kant, *Werke*, VII, ed. Weischedel, Darmstadt, 1968).
[13] *Loc. cit.*, p. 680.
[14] See also, e.g., Karl Löwith, "Ins Christliche übersetzt: Wir sind allesamt Sünder, es ist keiner, der gerecht ist".—On the revolution of attitudes demanded by Kant: "Christlich gesagt: Es bedarf dazu einer Wiedergeburt", in "Die Beste aller Welten und das radikal Böse im Menschen", from *Vorträge und Abhandlungen. Zur Kritik der christlichen Überlieferung* (Stuttgart, 1966), p. 194.   [15] Kant, *op. cit.*, p. 686.

that evil "originates in time". He sees its origin within reason. He regarded the theory of original sin as singularly inappropriate. Evil cannot be inherited from one's predecessors; rather should every individual evil act be seen as man's unmediated fall from the state of innocence. To look at this any other way would be to restrict the freedom of moral action.[16]

The possibility of making the step from evil to good remains just as puzzling as the origin of evil. Outside aids, such as grace, must be rigorously excluded: "What man is in the moral sense, or ought to become, good or evil, is something he makes, or has made, *himself*."[17] If the moral law says we must become better people, then it must be possible for us to do so: you can because you ought. This demand is fundamental to our moral constitution. The necessary change of heart is not merely a matter of reforming exterior behaviour, but requires a revolution within our mental attitudes. But ultimately, both the fall into evil and the subsequent conversion to the good transcend our understanding. The struggle between the good and the evil principle, Kant goes on to say, should result in victory for the good and the establishment "of God's Kingdom on earth". This idea of a human moral community implies that evil has a social as well as an individual quality.

No matter how great the oppression of evil, Kant seeks and recognizes grounds for hope.[18] However, his theory of evil has ambivalent aspects. He would rather admit perplexity than through careless speculation put forward pseudo-solutions. In spite of the contradictions, the solution must lie within the area Kant mapped out, for any other explanation would have disastrous consequences for his theory of practical reason.

Oelmüller has also adverted to this unresolved contradiction. Carefully referring to a "hypothesis" for an explanation of evil, he writes: "It fails, however, on the basis of the distinction between the intelligible and empirical character of man developed from the standpoint of transcendental philosophy, to make sense of the connection between the intelligible act and the experiences

[16] Cf. Kant, *op. cit.*, p. 690.
[17] Kant, *op. cit.*, p. 694: according to Kant grace requires a preceding and characteristic activity of its own.
[18] Cf. Oelmüller, *op. cit.*, pp. 113-58, 212, 215.

of evil in time and history."[19] The problem of evil reveals a fundamental dilemma in Kant's philosophy. Even his *Critique of Pure
Reason* does not quite successfully overcome the dichotomy between an idea and a category, between the ego and the physical
world, and between the intelligible and empirical realms. In the
end, the concepts proper to the matter itself are still external: "In
so far as the form of cognition is indifferent to the content of what
is cognized, it is contingent. It is the matter that understanding
ought to grasp; and the matter is the purpose external to the understanding itself, on which its being is grounded."[20]

In practical philosophy, the moral world is similarly the product of the moral will; Kant's subject is the citizen who determines good and bad order through what he does. Though in this
process the autonomy, freedom and self-affirmation of the individual are for Kant the dominant ideas, there is still a residue
of instrumentalism in cognition and will. The elements of the
apparatus of transcendental cognition, categories and forms of
intuition, as well as the subject-possessor of free will, remain ultimately beyond history, the development of science, and society.
The "you can because you ought" is an imperious charge; the
"pitiless majesty" of the moral law had already appeared to
Schiller as the possible foundation for a new condition of slavery:
human nature beneath the yoke of a relentlessly demanding
moral law.

Both these consequences, and the division between morality
and sensibility, to which Kant's whole intention runs counter,[21]
culminate in the *aporia* of evil. The evident givenness of evil, its

[19] *Op. cit.*, p. 236. If anywhere, then it is here that the sentence from
the Preface to the *Critique of Pure Reason* can be applied: "I should suspend knowledge in order to make room for faith"; whether this is a weakness in Kant's position or a legitimate openness in his philosophy towards
Christian tradition is not now in discussion; for political theology (in the
critical sense), however, it does at least contain some important insights;
cf. Oelmüller, *op. cit.*, p. 20.

[20] M. Horkheimer, "Kants Philosophie und die Aufklärung", in *Zur
Kritik der instrumentalen Vernunft* (Frankfurt, 1967), p. 210.

[21] Cf. D. Henrich (ed.), Kant, Gentz, Rehberg, *Über Theorie und Praxis*
(Frankfurt, 1967). Henrich confirms (pp. 14 ff.) that in this book, at least,
theory extends beyond an instrumental relationship to practice; the ambivalent assessment of the French Revolution shows, however, the extent to
which the theory-practice problems remains unresolved.

crude facticity, refuses to be subsumed under the moral law.
Human nature—in Kant's philosophy a dumb stage-property—
announces its presence by refusing respect for a moral law bind-
ing on all rational beings. The moral categories of the Kantian
system fail at this point because that exists that should not exist.

While Kant, in order to avoid mythical, biological or pseudo-
speculative origin accounts, denied that evil could originate in
time, Marx could see its origin nowhere else (even if reason does
play a substantial part). Instead of a revolution in moral attitudes
as the source of hope in the good, Marx envisages a material and
social revolution as a means of ridding the world of evil. Against
Hegel, and to a lesser extent Kant, Marx indicates the contradiction of dismembered reality as opposed to a rationality that remains exterior to it. In this way, he faces up to the dilemma that
confronted Kant in connection with the facticity of evil.

The trans-empirical "I" is seen in the context of its own prac-
tice-relatedness; like Feuerbach's "religious sentiment", the autonomous subject of bourgeois philosophy also overlooks the fact
that it "is itself a social product, and that the abstract individual
whom he analyses belongs to a particular form of society".[22] Man
is not an abstract datum but an ensemble of social relationships:
"All the mysteries which lead theory towards mysticism find their
rational solution in human practice and in the comprehension of
this practice."[23] In place of the individual person creating his
world through cognition, there comes the producer who through
competitive labour personally controls the process of the historical
production of man and truth. This is not intended to refute
Kant's programme but to extend and concretize it. Evil here appears in structural form in the shape of alienated labour in which
man is equated with his products. Society suffers from this evil
not because of some prehistoric or supra-empirical accident, but
because of man as historical fact whose causes and effects are
humanly soluble because human in origin. The solution is to be

[22] Karl Marx, *Thesen ad Feuerbach*, Thesis 7, quoted from English translation in *Karl Marx—Selected Writings in Sociology and Philosophy*, ed.
T. B. Bottomore and M. Rubel (Penguin, 1969).
[23] Marx, *op. cit.*, Thesis 8.

achieved through revolutionizing the conditions which necessarily promote and prolong the rise of evil.

For this reason, if for no other, says Marx, the free acceptance of moral law cannot lead to fundamental change: the autonomy of the individual implied in it has itself become ideological. For Marx, therefore, Kant's theory remains essentially one about practice in which the contradiction of evil becomes to some extent the antagonism of practice towards theory. Marx starts from this situation, observes the weaknesses in theory and practice by playing one off against the other, and forces a reconciliation in the critique of ideology and revolution. Evil then appears as a transitory problem; ridding the world of temporal and concrete evil takes precedence over anything else, including a discussion of the nature of evil.

But, as is well known, Marx too had to admit the weaknesses in his system: in *Capital* there are some heavily pessimistic passages in which he recognizes the inevitability of a remaining residue of force and work that might have serious consequences for the "realm of freedom": "With this development the realm of natural necessity expands . . . nevertheless, this always remains a realm of necessity. Beyond it begins that development of human potentiality for its own sake, the true realm of freedom, which however can only flourish upon that realm of necessity as its basis."[24] Too late now to talk of a problem-free appropriation of nature through revolution, or man's identity with himself and nature. At this point, and in contrast to the more usual opinions, Marx looks more like a pessimist;[25] this is probably the point at which to explain the connection between some neo-Marxists and Schopenhauer and the literature of pessimism.[26]

However appropriate and applicable might be the description of the social structure of evil indicted by Marx, and however important it might be that ridding the world of concrete evil should take precedence over a definitive solution of the question of the

[24] *Das Kapital*, III (Berlin, 1953), pp. 873 ff. (English translation quoted from Bottomore, *op. cit.*, note 22 above).

[25] Thus A. Schmidt, "Der Begriff der Natur in der Lehre von Marx", in *Frankfurter Beiträge zur Soziologie*, 11 (Frankfurt, 1962), p. 118.

[26] Cf. M. Horkheimer, "Die Aktualität Schopenhauers", in *Kritik der instrumentalen Vernunft, op. cit.*, pp. 248–68.

origin of evil pure and simple, the Marxist categories remain inadequate when it is a matter of discussing the remnants of alienation that even the realm of freedom contains. It seems logical to attempt a solution to this problem partly through a strongly mechanistic (Engels, dialectical materialism) or romantic (Bloch) dialectics of nature or history of nature, and partly through a problematicization of the nature-history relation as a whole. The tension between neo-Marxist thought and the positivist theory of knowledge in Germany—comparable with the structuralism debate in France—led to a stage where not only the nature of advanced capitalist societies as based on exchange value was seen as the very structure of evil, but where the same was said of the technological or structuralist mode of thinking itself, because it required an uncritical acceptance of historically conditioned forms of socialization. To the extent that cognition was thereby made only a rationality of ends-and-means, and thought merely the transcendental sign of applied knowledge, rationality was reduced to technology and became the handmaid of technocratic domination. In this instrumentalist approach, thought itself takes on an evil form; it becomes an evil that the individual is hardly able to withstand, because evil structures are difficult to comprehend and, through a process of internalization, readily establish themselves in man. Only in acts of selfless spontaneity, such as in love, and in a permanent state of self-critical reflection, can the individual break through the evil that surrounds him.

However, this critique of the technological mode of thought gets at only half the truth: since Francis Bacon, the self-critical reflection of empirical science has shown not only that even technology has some liberating aspects—in so far as it is anti-dogmatic[27]—but that, in the concern with methodology shown by the various sciences, there is an acknowledgment of the need not to ignore a persisting surplus of problems.[28]

It looks, therefore, as though the question of evil is making a

[27] Cf. on this. Jürgen Habermas, Technik und Wissenschaft als Ideologie (Frankfurt, 1968), esp. pp. 104–45.

[28] Cf. E. Topitsch (ed.), Logik der Sozialwissenschaften (Cologne-Berlin, 1967); H. Albert, Traktat über kritische Vernunft (Tübingen, 1968); A. Wellmer, Kritische Gesellschaftstheorie und Positivismus (Frankfurt, 1969); Th. W. Adorno, et al., Der Positivismusstreit in der deutschen Soziologie (Neuwied & Berlin, 1969).

fresh appearance in scientific theory—but in methodological dress. However, the arguments latterly deduced are clearly obsolete because of the scientific-problematical terms in which they are carried on, even with regard to the problem of evil. The answers are too tentative. The proper approach, following Kant and Marx, is to let the question "Why evil?" rest, in favour of furthering the struggle against the historical and concrete manifestations of evil and making this the dominant concern of all the sciences.

Translated by Mark Hollebone

Fergus Kerr

The Problem of Moral Decision in Contemporary English Philosophy: A Survey

THE question to which this paper is addressed is whether and how the problem of moral decision is envisaged and assessed in the work of representative practitioners of the linguistic-analytical style of philosophy which predominates in the English-speaking world. Do such philosophers take the phenomenon of evil seriously, as seriously as any imaginable Christian interpretation of the human situation would seem to demand; or do they rather trivialize the phenomenon of evil by a technique of over-subtle and pseudo-neutral investigation of the grammar of what people say of evil in ordinary language?

Two preliminary observations should be made briefly. In the first place, it is surely not to philosophers of any school that an educated man would turn in search of insight into the phenomenon of evil. He would rather read the great novelists or go to the theatre. The novels of Dostoevski and Henry James, the tales of D. H. Lawrence, the plays of Shakespeare in current production in London and Stratford—those are the sources of serious reflection on the nature of evil and a philosopher who ignores such data condemns himself to mere speculation. As far as the English-speaking world is concerned, surely the most illuminating contemporary discussion of the problem of evil is taking place in the continuing debate about the nature of tragedy. To compare, for instance, George Steiner, *The Death of Tragedy* (1961), with Raymond Williams, *Modern Tragedy* (1966), and to study the critique of the latter by Walter Stein, *Criticism as Dialogue* (1969), would be to begin to understand what it is like to practise complex and sophisticated reflection about evil and choice. It is even possible that it is in thinking of this kind that the most intractable problems in human life, such as the problem of evil and the morality of decision, become most accessible. It is at all events not in academic philosophy that profound thinking on such matters is taking place at the present time, at least in the English-speaking world. But one must not conclude from this that no profound thinking is taking place on such matters.

The second observation is the obvious one that even in the English-speaking world there are many more ways of doing philosophy than the predominant one. In the domains of ethics and philosophy of religion, as it happens, the variety of approaches is considerably greater than elsewhere. It is, of course, unfair to lump philosophers together in the way which we are going to do for the purposes of this article: there are, after all, profound disagreements and real arguments even among philosophers who have the discipline of the linguistic-analytical approach in common and regard it as the only valid way of doing philosophy; but a survey cannot be very discriminating.

Surveys of the whole field there are of course already. Mention should certainly be made of Mary Warnock's *Ethics since 1900* (1960, 1966²), the best starting-point for a study of how English-speaking philosophers approach moral problems. The book begins with a chapter on the style of metaphysical ethics which prevailed in British philosophy in the late nineteenth century. F. H. Bradley is treated in some detail as typical: "It was Bradley's Hegelian idealist ethical theory which dominated the beginning of the century, and it is against this background that the later developments must be seen" (*op. cit.*, p. 10). The next chapter deals with the work of G. E. Moore, particularly his most important and influential book, *Principia Ethica* (1903). It is not difficult to show how the style and argument of this book made it impossible for subsequent philosophers to think in terms of trying like Bradley to deduce a theory of ethics from some general explanatory theory of the nature of reality at large. This is the point at which ethics broke loose from metaphysics. From here onwards it has seemed possible to discuss evil and responsibility without reference to ontological questions. Of the next phase in the history of moral philosophy the most typical examples are W. D. Ross, *The Right and the Good* (1930), and H. A. Pritchard, *Moral Obligation* (1949). The work of such philosophers is now usually described as *intuitionism*: "The demand for proof of the truth of ultimate moral intuitions is as nonsensical as the demand for proof in the case of genuine knowledge. Once you have got a moral intuition, it is impossible to doubt what it is that you have; and anything in terms of which you tried to prove its truth would be necessarily less certain than the intuition itself" (*op. cit.*, p. 43).

The meaning of ethical terms resides, for the intuitionists, in some immediate recognition of the quality of rightness, in some direct intuition of goodness. The argument here is principally over how much or how little may be expected of such intuition. It was among such moralists that A. J. Ayer's *Language, Truth and Logic* burst like a bombshell in 1936. In his famous chapter 6 (twenty pages in which ethics and theology are both disposed of) Ayer contends that any statement which has meaning must fall into one or other of two categories. Either it must be *analytic*: necessarily true but not concerned with empirical matters of fact; or it must be *empirical*. If it is empirical, it can never be more than probable; it is a hypothesis. Both the meaning and the probability of the hypothesis are established by empirical verification. If a statement is to qualify for the second category, then, it must be patent of verification by sense-experience. The point is that no statement can be said to have any meaning which is not either analytic or verifiable by observation of the world. The propositions of logic and mathematics fall into the first category; the propositions of science and of ordinary life, in so far as these state matters of fact, fall into the second category. There are no other possible categories. Ethical propositions, then, fall into neither of these categories. They are not simply analytic: they do not, in Ayer's words, "simply record our determination to use symbols in a certain fashion". On the other hand, it is not plausible to say that ethical propositions are open to verification by ordinary sense-experience. Even an intuitionist does not claim to have sense-experience of goodness.

Ayer goes on to outline the theory of ethics which is now known as *emotivism*: "If I say to someone 'you acted wrongly in stealing that money', I am not stating anything more than if I had simply said 'you stole that money'. In adding that this action is wrong I am simply evincing my moral disapproval of it." The point here is, then, that ethical propositions are simply expressions of feeling, they are in no sense cognitive. Ayer makes one remark which is worth quoting: "It is worth mentioning that ethical terms do not serve only to express feeling. They are calculated also to arouse feeling, and so to stimulate action. Indeed some of them are used in such a way as to give the sentences in which they occur the effect of commands." This opening out of emotivism is important because it prepared the way for *prescriptivism*, the ethical theory represented most significantly by R. M. Hare, *The Language of Morals* (1952), *Freedom and Reason* (1963), which remains the dominant style of doing ethics in Oxford. Hare finds the specific quality of moral language by making a distinction betwen prescriptive and descriptive language. He says that prescriptive language is imperative, in that it tells us to do this or that. It is not hard to see that Hare's ethics displays a Kantian fascination with the model of the imperative.

A similar account of the history of modern ethics is given by G. J. Warnock, *Contemporary Moral Philosophy* (1967), and by Alasdair Macintyre, *A Short History of Ethics* (1966). It is also worth referring to Kai Nielsen's contribution to the article on ethics in *The Encyclopedia of Philosophy* (1967), where a more detailed survey is to be found along with extensive bibliographies. He makes the crucial distinction between two fundamental positions in ethics, *naturalism* and *non-naturalism*, *teleology* and *deontology*. We may say that naturalistic theories of ethics relate values to reality by defining the good and related notions in terms of observable criteria, such as fulfilment of natural desire (Aristotle, Thomas Aquinas), production of pleasure for the greatest number (hedonistic utilitarianism), relevance to historical progress (Marx) or efficiency of means to ends (pragmatism). Non-naturalistic theories of ethics, on the other hand, insist that the meaning of ethical language goes beyond the observable facts on which ethical judgments are grounded, and they look for the meaning outside nature. The intuitionists, as we have already noted, found the meaning of ethical language in some immediate recognition of goodness. The emotivists and the prescriptivists, in the end, are proponents of non-cognitive theories, and in this they come interestingly close to certain existentialist theories of ethics. There is, in fact, a good deal more similarity between English-speaking and European-continental philosophers than is often admitted. This is particularly evident in the field of ethical theory.

Besides the work of R. M. Hare, mention should be made of P. H. Nowell-Smith, *Ethics* (1954), Bernard Mayo, *Ethics & the Moral Life* (1958), Alan Montefiore, *A Modern Introduction to Moral Philosophy* (1959) and John Hartland-Swann, *An Analysis of Morals* (1960). These constitute the essential documents in linguistic-analytical theory of ethics. It should be noted that they all represent the precipitate of personal investigation and lectures now at least ten or fifteen years old; and current work in the philosophical journals is mostly critique of these ideas.

The similarity between this sort of ethics and existentialist ethics has ben observed by Iris Murdoch, *Sartre: Romantic Rationalist* (1955). Our attention is drawn by Kai Nielsen (*op. cit.*) to four contentions basic to linguistic-analytical ethics and also in existentialist ethics. In the first place, it is taken for granted that Moore was right in his arguments against what he called the naturalistic fallacy: moral statements cannot be deduced from any other sorts of statements, whether biological, historical, psychological, sociological, ontological or religious. There is something unique about moral language. It is important to insist on this: while of course it means that ethics is regarded as somehow autonomous, being independent of any metaphysics, it means at the same time that ethics can never be reduced to anything other than itself. English moralists are neither behaviourists nor positivists, whatever may be said to the contrary by some of their critics. They remain in this respect thoroughly Kantian. In the second place, it is a basic contention that no moral choice or question of value can be guaranteed by logical rules. Thirdly, we are free, so far as language or logic is concerned, to apply evaluative or prescriptive terms to anything we wish to commend or condemn, criticize or approve, prescribe or forbid. Fourthly and finally, moral utterances are generalizable decisions, resolutions or subscriptions.

What is fundamental to the work of a philosopher like Hare is the insistence that there must be some moral principles which are not derivable from any other principles, moral or otherwise, historical or theological, sociological or metaphysical. Being fundamental moral principles, they are not even verifiable in principle. Such principles articulate moral commitments and can have no justification other than themselves. They require no ground for what is deemed worthy of acceptance depends ultimately on the commitments themselves: the generalizable commitments, decisions, resolutions or subscriptions which an agent is willing to make. Critics tend to argue that such an ethics rests on a deep irrationalism which in effect destroys the possibility of a normative and therefore rational ethics. There is an interesting difference of approach here in how linguistic-analytical moralists would respond to this critique. To say that moral principles are simply expressions of choice and articulations of commitment is of course to say that we cannot simply discover what is good or evil and that we cannot know *a priori* that some course of action is to be pursued. On the contrary, we must create our own values. What we in fact do, generates our morals; our behaviour is always committed, and moral principles are simply the articulation of this commitment.

But if this is so, for linguistic-analytical moralists, it is not a dramatic feature of the human condition, it is not a situation that provokes *angst*. It is simply a conceptual truth about the nature of moral discourse. As Kai Nielsen says (*op. cit.*): "It is not a fact of the human condition that man is born into a world alien and indifferent to human purposes. What is a fact is that the phrases 'the universe has a purpose' and 'value and being are one' are unintelligible phrases. To say 'man creates his own values' is in reality only to say in a dramatic way that a judgment of value is an expression of choice. This statement, it is argued, is not an anguished cry of the human heart but is merely an expression of a linguistic convention." In other words, to say that *ens et bonum convertuntur* is a meaningless assertion is not to opt for some melodramatic existentialist philosophy of the absurd; it is not to say that any choice at all is justified, it is not to say that anything is permissible or that all human actions are of equal value; it is not to adopt nihilism. Such statements as these, that anything is permissible or that all human actions are of equal value, are themselves value judgments; they could not follow from the claim that judgments of value are expressions of choice, because this claim is not itself a statement of value but a meta-ethical statement about the meaning of ethical statements: one cannot derive an "ought" from an "is" (the original claim of David Hume, accepted by Kant, as central in Hare as in Sartre).

To sum up so far, then, we may say this. Behind English-speaking philosophers at the present time lie the intuitionists: in reaction against post-Hegelian metaphysicizing ethics the intuitionists made moral language *sui generis*; they argued that fundamental moral concepts are simply indefinable; they claimed that fundamental moral judgments were simply, transparently and not further explicably, self-evident. As G. J. Warnock says: "Moral truths were, it seemed, such that nothing could possibly be said about what they meant, what their grounds were, or even why they mattered at all." The reaction to this was emotivism: an attempt to seek foundations for moral judgments but only by reducing them to something else, to expressions of approval or disapproval, to articulations of emotion. This developed into prescriptivism: an attempt to focus on the nature of moral utterances, to see them as a sort of prescriptive discourse very like imperatives. And this offers points of comparison with existentialist ethics: it shows how central the notion of choice, of commitment, is in such moralists as Hare; and it indicates the sort of criticism which is now being made. The most fundamental discontent with Hare's ethical theory is that it seems to make moral language groundless and arbitrary. As Nowell-Smith says, criticizing Hare from a position very sympathetic to his, "nothing that we discover about the nature of moral judgments entails that it is wrong to put all Jews in gas-chambers".

It is not to our purpose here to go through the details of Hare's argument. We want to stress only that the notion of choice, the concept of decision, is the central preoccupation of Hare's ethics (moral utterances are commitments). This concentration on the nature of decision goes with a certain disregard for the justification of moral decision. It is a criticism from within the linguistic-analytical school that Hare's stress on decision verges on an irrational *decisionism*. And even if the whole style of his argument is undramatic and nonchalant, it seems fairly clear that the final meaning of his position is not unlike that of certain existentialists. Hare argues that his thesis about the logical status of moral language does not commit him to the position that there can be no rational discussion and resolution of conflicts in moral principle. But philosophers who criticize him, again for instance Nowell-Smith, suggest that he has a far too Protestant conception of moral language. They suggest that Hare seems in the end to have recourse to some private experience of what is to count as a moral claim. This runs counter to the post-Wittgensteinian insistence on the importance of having public criteria for any claim that is to be intelligible (and hence arguable and open to rational justification and resolution).

The main burden of the criticism, then, of the dominant style of English moral philosophy, is that it pays so much heed to the nature of moral decision that it neglects the problem of justifying moral decisions and tends to repeat the typically Kantian impasse. As Alasdair Macintyre says: "Hare's prescriptivism is, in the end, a re-issue of the view that behind my moral evaluations there is not and cannot be any greater authority than that of my own choices. To understand evaluative concepts is to understand that our use of these concepts does not of itself commit us to any particular set of moral beliefs. The criteria for true belief in matters of fact are independent of our choices; but our evaluations are governed by no criteria but those which we ourselves choose to impose upon them. This is a repetition of Kant's view of the moral subject as law-giver; but it makes him an arbitrary sovereign who is the author of the law that he utters, and who constitutes it law by uttering it in the form of a universal prescription" (*op. cit.*, p. 262). A de-theologized Kantian imperativism: that is the basic feature of contemporary British ethical theory.

What is there to be said, then, about the problem of moral evil and of decision? It has to be admitted that there has been very little discussion of evil by contemporary moralists in the Oxford tradition. The only context in which there has been notable debate is in that of theodicy: see J. L. Mackie, "God and Omnipotence", *Mind* (April 1955), and Antony Flew, "Divine Omnipotence and Human Freedom", *New Essays in Philosophical*

Theology (1955), and the critical comment on these two articles by Ninian Smart: "Omnipotence, Evil and Supermen", *Philosophy* (April 1961), with the replies in the same journal by Flew (January 1962) and Mackie (April 1962). Attention should also be directed to the work of John Hick, *God and Evil* (1966), but this is an old-fashioned essay in philosophy of religion, displaying no more than general sympathy with linguistic-analytical styles of thinking. The plain truth is that the problem of evil has not attracted the attention of any contemporary English moralist, at least in that form. It is still the case, as Iris Murdoch pointed out in 1955, that the Oxford moralist's moral world seems to exclude certain conflicts altogether: referring to Gilbert Ryle's famous book she writes: "The 'world' of *The Concept of Mind* is the world in which people play cricket, cook cakes, make simple decisions, remember their childhood and go to the circus; not the world in which they commit sins, fall in love, say prayers or join the Communist Party." The illustrations which Oxford philosophers use, in fact, come from a world in which nothing so disturbing as the phenomenon of evil seems ever to enter.

There is more than one explanation for this. The apology which would be offered by a sympathizer would be to the effect that it is important to get clear about small matters before one tackles the larger questions: it is more illuminating to see how decisions work in uncomplicated instances than it is to focus on extreme situations. But this obviously contains a whole experience of being human—others would think that it is only by reflecting on dramatic situations that one can take the full measure of what it is to be human: "O the mind, mind has mountains; cliffs of fall/Frightful, sheer, no-man-fathomed. Hold them cheap/May who ne'er hung there" (G. M. Hopkins).

While it must be admitted, then, that the problem of evil excites little or no attention from contemporary English philosophers, it is clear that the notion of decision is a central concern of moralists such as we have mentioned. So far as the techniques of linguistic analysis go, it is obviously too difficult to demonstrate how they work apart from giving some rigorous discussion of particular concepts. There has been lively discussion of the free-will problem, for example, and what seems to be new and promising is this. In the past, among traditional philosophers, it seems that attempts to solve the free-will problem have centred round the problem of whether concepts related to human action name events which result wholly from antecedent causal chains of the sort described by physical science and, if so, whether this fact is compatible with moral responsibility. What has been questioned, in the linguistic-analytical tradition, is this presupposition: is it so evident that any concept which is related to human action is the name of an event or series of events? To look closely at how we actually use such concepts as "choosing", "deciding" and "doing" may make us doubt this. In effect, that is to say, there is a whole group of fundamental problems in ethical theory which centre on the relation between minds and bodies. The tendency here is to argue that some words which we ordinarily think of as describing private mental acts or events can be made sense of without mentioning mental acts. It is argued that one can show that such concepts as "choose", "decide" and "intend" can be explicated either in terms of publicly observable physical events or in terms of tendencies for such events to occur. Here should be mentioned the work of G. E. M. Anscombe, *Intention* (1958), P. T. Geach, *Mental Acts* (1957), and Stuart Hampshire, *Thought and Action* (1959).

And there is a second group of problems which attract much attention in the technical journals at the present time: such problems as how it is that we determine the boundary between an action and what precedes it, as well as between an action and what follows it—problems then of causality, motivation, result and consequence. Though these analyses have not so far been systematized to form any general theory (few English moralists would attempt anything so ambitious), it is clearly recognized that they are of crucial importance to any attempt to resolve the dispute between formalist ethical theories, which judge individual actions by rules alone, and teleological theories, which judge actions by consequences alone. Reference should be made to D. M. Mackinnon, *A Study in Ethical Theory* (1957), where an attempt is made to go beyond *Gesinnungsethik* and *Erfolgsethik*, by asking finally whether the problem of the possibility of metaphysics may not after all have some bearing on the way we think we should live, choose and act.

Behind all these efforts looms the figure of Ludwig Wittgenstein: it is only within the last ten years that the implications of
his work for ethics have begun to be explored. It is too early to
offer a report, but it is surely permissible to conclude that, for all
its modesty and narrowness, a philosophical tradition in which
Wittgenstein's work is influential cannot remain permanently un-
touched by a sense of urgency about thinking and living seriously.

Thomas Berry

The Problem of Moral Evil and Guilt in Early Buddhism

ACCORDING to Buddhist teaching man lives in a universe that is thoroughly moral in its structure. There was no beginning of the existing order of things, but the determinations of reality such as we know them were brought about by responsible human deeds, even though these deeds were done under the influence of an all-pervading lack of understanding known as *avidya*. By continuing life in this condition man is hindered from attaining the transcendent experience of *nirvana*, he is bound more tightly to the painful world of unending cyclic change, he is tormented inwardly, he is alienated from other men, and finally he merits a punishment which is designated as a state of ruin, of affliction, and destruction of himself as a man, a state known as *vinipata* or *niraya*. The absolute evil which results from moral misconduct is continued existence in the endless series of births and rebirths in a world of death, grief, mourning, pain, sorrow and despair. The absolute good is liberation from this cycle into the experience of *nirvana*.

The difficulty of the moral life of man was clearly recognized by Buddha. This difficulty is found both in the surrounding world and in man himself. The world is not the manifestation of divine goodness. It is rather a meaningless succession of changing phenomena resulting from limitless ignorance and causing endless suffering. But if the world is in such a condition the deeper cause must be found in man. Whatever the cause, Buddhism wished to face the situation in its true reality. At few moments in history has any tradition sought to face so directly the overwhelming obstacles that man experiences in his efforts at moral rectitude. It is precisely its awareness of this difficulty that makes the Buddhist commitment to the morally responsible deed so impressive. Everything in Buddhism begins with this searching analysis of the human situation, the difficulty yet the possibility of attaining a moral goodness leading to a liberating experience. The struggle involves teaching, understanding, and spiritual training. But if man does not attain the liberating experience he is himself responsible for his failure.

The basic difficulty is lack of understanding. This leads to the disordered functioning of the sense organs and their contact with the phenomenal world, then to a craving for experiences in the sense order and desire for the possession of things, with a consequent emotional entanglement difficult to overcome. Finally comes attachment to individual temporal existence, assertion of the phenomenal self. This craving, clinging, attachment, are often described as a fire which inflames the entire being of man. Body, feeling, perception, the activities and consciousness itself are all on fire: "Ablaze with what? Ablaze with sensuous desire, with ill-feeling, with foolish attachment, with birth, disintegration and death, with sorrow, mourning, suffering, and despair."[1]

Ten fetters, born of this intense inner craving, bind man to the endless wheel of becoming. These include belief in an abiding self, an unsettled mind, attachment to external rules and ritual, sensuous desire, antagonism, a yearning for the realm of forms or absence of forms, egotism, impatience, and ignorance. Of these the first five bind man to the world of sensation. The other five bind man to the realm of his emotional and intellectual existence. Along with these forms of affliction, these fetters, which involve man in evil action, there are the deadly *asavas*, the intoxicants, defilements, cankers, or destructive attitudes deep in the being of man which confuse the mind and absorb it into wrong-doing. These are not physical but moral-emotional disorientations. Because they overwhelm man so completely they are also called "floods" and "yokes". As floods they are "conditions which submerge in a continuous cycle of birth and rebirth the persons in whom they have a dominance". These *asavas* are often numbered

[1] *Samyutta Nikaya of the Sutta Pitaka*, ed. M. Leon Feer, Parts I–V (London, Henry Frowde, 1884–98). Reprint (London, 1960), IV, 20.

as three: sense-delight, attachment to becoming, and ignorance. Sometimes a fourth, attachment to mental attitudes, is added.

Because of this formidable array of forces within man and in his life situation, the problem arises as regards man's moral responsibility for his actions; whether he could do anything about his life or whether he is caught in a fatal entanglement whence there is no effective way of escape. This point was argued out by a number of spiritual leaders in India throughout the sixth century B.C. The one most firm in his rejection of moral controls over life, and the one most consistently opposed by Buddha, was Makkhali Gosala who asserted that fate, *niyati*, so dominated the world that man could do nothing effective to remedy his sorrowful situation. To an inquiry made of him he answered: "There is, O king, no cause either remote or immediate for the moral wickedness of beings; they become wicked without reason or cause. Nor is there any cause remote or immediate for the moral goodness of beings; they become good without reason or cause. The acquisition of any condition or moral quality depends neither on one's own deeds or on the deeds of another, nor on any human effort whatsoever. There is no such thing as moral power or energy or human strength or vigour. All things, all living beings, all souls, since they are without force, power, or energy of their own, are inclined one way or another by their fate (*niyati*), by their inherited qualities, by their individual natures; and according to their place in the order of the sixfold classification of mankind they experience pleasure or pain."[2] During a vast period of time both the fools and wise men pass on their way through their due cycles of transmigration. Nor can either by any exercise of virtue or penance resolve the problems which men face. Comfort and pain, good and evil are fixed with a determination that cannot be altered: "Just as a ball of cord will unwind just so far and no farther, so both the wise and the foolish pass through the cycle of repeated births and deaths for a certain determined period of time and only then attain release from sorrow."[3]

This is the most forceful position taken at this time against the capacity of man to deal with his human situation. It is also the

[2] *Digha Nikaya*, ed. T. W. Rhys Davids and J. Estlin Carpenter, 3 vols. (London, 1889-1911). Reprint (London, 1949), I, 53.
[3] *Ibid.*, I, 54.

most depressing since it proposed that not even virtue could bring to man release from the agony he experiences in his own being. This Buddha answered with an argument of experience rather than with any speculative refutation. The argument proposed by Gosala had been addressed to a king who was inquiring concerning the visible results of a life of virtue such as that attained by the monks in their places of retirement. Buddha's argument was that virtue is possible and that it does bring about release from the intense agony that man experiences within his own self, for this agony is not something extrinsic to the moral life but the immediate intrinsic consequence of the good or evil deeds done by men in this world. Attainment of an interior state of bliss is an absolute necessity in the Buddhist programme of moral development because it provided the motivation of the life of virtue. The *Dhammapada*, one of the most significant of all statements of Buddhist thought, presents very clearly the proposition that suffering follows the evil thought, speech, or deed "just as the wheel follows the foot of the ox that draws the cart", and also that happiness follows upon a good thought, speech, or deed as "a shadow that never departs".[4]

Thus, in answering Gosala, Buddha recounted to the king the case of a slave who recognizes the high spiritual calling of the monk and gives himself over to a life of high moral virtue. His detachment from things of the physical and sense order brings him to "a feeling of serenity wherein nothing evil can enter".[5] Beyond that he attains a wonderful freedom and joy: "Just as though someone in prison after being granted his liberty and restoration of his possessions would be joyful of heart."[6] Thence he would pass on to a profound peace and inward recollection wherein he would experience a rebirth in a higher order of reality: "Just, O king, as if a person were so covered from his head to his feet in a pure white garment so that there would be no part of his body not inclosed in that pure white garment, even so does the new mendicant sit there so permeated with a feeling of purity, of radiance, of inwardness that there would be no place in his whole being not suffused with that feeling of purity."[7]

[4] *Dhammapada*, ed. Suriyagoda Simangala Thera (London, 1914), verses I, 2.   [5] *Digha Nikaya*, I, 70.   [6] *Ibid.*, 72.   [7] *Ibid.*, 76.

The king, having heard this account of Buddha, confesses his guilt of the past and gives himself to the life of spiritual perfection. "Evil has conquered me, O Lord, enervated and foolish and wrong-minded as I am. For attaining kingship I executed my father, a good man, a good king! May the Blessed One receive me, Lord, for I admit it as a fault that in the future I may discipline myself." He is then accepted by Buddha, for according to custom whoever admits his failing as a failing and confesses it attains to self-discipline in the future.[8]

Buddhaghosa, the great Buddhist spiritual writer of the fifth century A.D., considers this same difficulty of the moral life in the opening section of his work, *Visuddhimagga, The Path of Purity*. He states the problem in terms of a tangle in a passage taken from an earlier scripture. Given the involvement of man in these vast determining forces of the world, a way of escape seems impossible: "The tangle within and the tangle without, mankind is entangled in a tangle. Thus I propose to Buddha this question: Who can untangle this tangle?"[9] He describes a tangle as a "maze of desires" and he compares it to the intertwining of branches in a bamboo cluster. Without in any manner diminishing the moral difficulty faced by man caught in this situation, Buddhaghosa affirms his conviction that man can overcome this difficulty with the basic moral resources that are available to man. By virtue, by intellectual awareness, and by spiritual insight, man can succeed in "untangling the tangle".

While the early Buddhists probed this deeply into the basic questions concerning moral guilt they gave no indication of yielding to any form of determinism. They held firmly both to the harsh reality of man's moral plight and to his power of moral decision. There are many words in the Buddhist language designating that which is morally evil and the corresponding guilt incurred by those who do such deeds. *Pāpa* is one of the more common words designating evil in a broad sense, but most often with a sense of moral guilt. *Akusala* is that which is not right or not good. *Vajja* designates that which ought to be avoided as a fault

[8] *Ibid.*, 85.
[9] *Visuddhimagga of Buddhaghosacariya*, ed. Henry Clarke Warren. Revised by Dharmananda Kosambi, Harvard University Press (1950), Part I, par. 1.

or a sin. *Apunna* is that which is not meritorious or what is non-virtuous. *Aparadha* indicates offence. Corresponding to descriptions of evil deeds there are descriptions of evil persons. An evil man is in darkness, is bound to a long succession of existences in which he will suffer constant affliction. Constantly there is the refrain: "Why do you not search for a light, you who are immersed in darkness?"[10] The deeds of the wicked man are like "a smouldering fire within him".[11] The man who abandons moral principle is "cruel, has blood on his hands, is set on harming and killing others, is merciless in his behaviour to living things. He is one who seizes what is not offered and he steals whatever is not given him both in the countryside and in the villages."[12] At the end of life he comes to perdition. Indeed those monks whose deeds, whose speech and thoughts are evil, who persecute the virtuous, fixed in their perverted views, involved in unjust actions, these men "at the dissolution of the body, arise in the desert, the bad end, the abyss, even to hell".[13] Such a person, decayed within and filled with lust, arouses only disgust and is to be avoided as "repulsive".

The first step in rescuing such a person from his evil situation is to awaken in him an awareness of the evil nature of his actions. This involves a sense of guilt. Then comes confession of guilt, and finally restoration to a state of goodness. Such is the pattern of reformation sought in Buddhism. This entire process of moral rectification originates in a stark confrontation with reality as it truly is. This includes insight into the nature and functioning of the phenomenal world, but especially an insight into the realities of man's own being. Of Buddha it was said: "By understanding the entire world just exactly as it is, he is released from the entire world and clings to nothing therein." All of this is reduced to a twofold proposition: "To perceive evil as evil is the first instruction. Then perceiving evil as evil, be repelled by it, be cleansed, be freed from it; this is the second instruction."[14] As soon as a

---

[10] *Dhammapada*, 60.

[11] *Ibid.*, 71.

[12] *Majjhima Nikaya*, ed. V. Trenckner and R. Chalmers, 3 vols. (London, 1888–99). Reprint (London, 1964), I, 286.

[13] *Ibid.*, I, 287.

[14] *Iti-Vuttaka*, ed. Ernst Windisch (London, 1889). Reprint (London, 1948), p. 33.

man could see his impending destruction through evil he was expected to turn from it. He was also expected to manifest a guilt feeling for his situation, for submitting to the attractions of his senses or of his inner faculties. This admission of guilt supposed personal responsibility: "If because of slothfulness, sir, you did not perform that which is good in deed, speech, or thought, they will certainty treat you in accord with your slothfulness. For this wicked deed is your own. It was not done by your mother or father, by brother, sister, friends or acquaintances, nor by any friend or relative, or by ascetics or Brahmans, or by any deities. This wicked deed was done by you. You will yourself suffer its consequences."[15]

When an offence has been committed the person experiences an inner affliction: "He is terrified at his awareness: 'I have failed to do what is virtuous in deed, speech or thought.' Therefore he is afflicted at such a thought."[16] Often there is mention of being tormented by remorse and shame, *ottappa* and *hiri*. These two are often mentioned together when speaking of an awareness of guilt. They are considered the two basic forces that ensure the safety of the world. If these two did not "protect the world" it would fall into a state of total confusion.[17] A description of a bad conscience is given in the *Book of Monastic Discipline* at the failure of a monk. In consequence of his remorse and shame, he became gaunt, wretched, discoloured; the veins showed on his body, he became deeply saddened, downcast, repentant, overwhelmed with grief.[18]

One of the most common events narrated in the Buddhist scriptures is confession of moral guilt. Confession of both moral and legal guilt takes place periodically within the Buddhist community. Every fortnight the list of faults is read aloud and each monk is expected to admit his guilt. If he does not admit guilt then he is further guilty of deliberate lying. To confess guilt is, on the other hand, to receive forgiveness and comfort. The essential thing is that the evil be recognized and confessed as evil.

[15] *Majjhima Nikaya*, III, 182.
[16] *Anguttara Nikaya*, ed. R. Morris and E. Hardy, 6 vols. (London, 1885–1910), I, 49.   [17] *Iti-Vuttaka*, 36.
[18] *Book of the Discipline*, tr. of *Vinayapitaka*, I. D. Horner, 4 vols. (London, 1949–51), I, 58.

The concept of guilt is somewhat mitigated in its expression since it is generally expressed in a phrase meaning to be overcome or defeated by an evil. The general word for transgression is *accaya*. This is most often used in the expression: *accayo mam accagama*, "an offence overcame me".

In all of this one can see how moral guilt is manifested and dealt with in early Buddhist tradition. Its firm commitment to moral responsibility led to an increasing emphasis on moral effort: "Monks, foster what is good. It can be accomplished. If this were something impossible I would not exhort you to do it. But since it is something that can be done, I exhort you: Cultivate that which is good."[19] The sixth step in the eightfold path of Buddhism is "right effort", *viriya*. We see this in the fervent exhortations so common in Buddhist practice: "Keep yourself from every evil deed: establish yourself in goodness; purify your thoughts. This is the message of the enlightened ones."[20] The last words of Buddha were concerned with this personal effort required to live a moral life: "I exhort you, brethren: Dissolution is inherent in all compounded reality! With earnestness, strive forward in virtue."[21] The monks, particularly, were not to give in to the conflict within them but were to struggle on towards the fulfilment of a good life while saying to themselves: "With delight would I see my skin and sinews and bones wither and my flesh and blood become wasted and shrivelled so long as I were able to keep firm in the path until I gain what may be gained by man's vigour, his effort, and his striving; for you also, monks, will soon reach that goal for which men abandon their households for the homeless life, attaining it for yourselves here in this life, and once having attained it, you will abide therein."[22]

[19] *Anguttara Nikaya*, I, 58.
[20] *Dhammapada*, 183.
[21] *Digha Nikaya*, II, 120.
[22] *Anguttara Nikaya*, I, 50.

José Luis Duhourq

The Presentation and Interpretation of Moral Evil in the Contemporary Cinema

IN the belief that concepts taken for granted in the world of the graphic image are likely to be not too familiar in theological circles, I have thought it proper to begin this study of one aspect of the contemporary cinema with a consideration of what it *is* at present, rather than just what it is *doing*.

I propose to study it from three angles: first, its technical potential, as an instrument of photographic reproduction; second, its expressive potential, as an art form which has now reached a sufficient degree of maturity to be studied as such; and finally, its place in contemporary culture as a linguistic form.

Where moral evil is concerned, I believe that the very concept is passing through a critical time, and I am taking for granted the fact that the notion of moral evil itself implies an interpretation of reality that has to take account of God, man and the world: to define these is to have defined the notion of moral evil.

I. THE ETHICAL IMPLICATIONS OF "REALISM" IN THE CONTEMPORARY CINEMA

Deducing the moral meaning of any expression of present-day culture supposes taking into account the process of mental change that is taking place all over the world, particularly since the end of the Second World War. There are two relevant aspects of this process that are sufficiently self-evident to be adduced without lengthy explanation: first, loss of confidence in the validity of both thought forms and physical structures hallowed by the

European tradition; second, the counterpart of the first, the movement of "liberalization" taken as the prerequisite for the establishment of a new existential truth. These two aspects have come together in a universally recognized moral quest—for "authenticity".

This authenticity lies behind a plethora of undertakings with greater or lesser degrees of validity, representing as it does a going beyond appearances in an attempt to reach the underlying reality of things and situations—to break them down into their molecular components, as it were. It is also behind the "objectivism" which has become dominant in contemporary narrative technique, thereby giving an ethical dimension that imperceptibly colours its products. This "objectivist vision" in fact carries a weight of "presentation" of its underlying experience. This is most convenient for consciences that have shaken off real or imagined restraints and yet feel the need for a solid and controllable basis of support.

In the cinema, this tendency—favoured by the tool of the trade, the camera—has, over the past twenty-five years, produced a "realism" which, despite the national and personal differences one would expect, constitutes a sufficiently coherent and homogeneous phenomenon for it to be taken as characteristic of the age. Whether it is called Italian neo-realism, French *nouvelle vague*, New York School or English Free Cinema, it shows the same features: rejection of all conventions (whatever the framework in which this rejection is expressed) and celebration of the mere fact of existence. The directors of this school forsake the studio for the open street, documenting everyday gestures, words and faces, in an effort to rediscover the ordinary and dignify it by the very fact of showing it. Although this documentary approach is not new in the history of the cinema, in these films it takes on a peculiar "prophetic" character through making people see *the same thing*, but in a different way, instead of bringing what is remote into focus.

This realism (and all other forms for that matter) can become morally problematical in so far as it does not always or necessarily subordinate the value of the manner of showing to the value of what is shown. In other words, the riches of phenomenological description for its own sake can attract the artist to such an extent that he no longer takes account of the fact that his closeness to his object can hinder his overall judgment by suppressing the perspective obtained by standing farther back. In practice, this can come to mean that the mere existence of a thing is taken as sufficient justification for showing it.

One does not have to be particularly clear-sighted to realize the dangers of this outlook. As a simple illustration of it in practice, take the cinematic representation of sexuality: after a phase of puritan repression it has now gone to the extreme where any erotic representation or possible aberration will find its exponent and defender.

A glance at the productions of the last few years will show two types of *realist*[1] approach: first, that of those whose view of life includes transcendence and selects and interprets facts in relation to it—Roberto Rossellini,[2] Robert Bresson, Carl Dreyer . . . ; and second, those who confine themselves to a demonstration of the situation of unhappiness and dissatisfaction in which so many men and women live today, presenting this as a consequence of deficient social, economic or religious structures—Michelangelo Antonioni, Claude Chabrol, Francesco Rossi, Tony Richardson, Maurizio Bellocchio. . . .

The first category, in admitting a concept of reality not based solely on what can be sensed and felt, accept the reference of the human conscience to a transcendent order. Moral evil for them is what the Christian calls sin. The others, generally speaking, merely follow the existential thought of this century. By interpreting it so well, however, they make themselves part of the quest for truth that underlies any philosophical search while at the same time associating themselves with a system that tends, explicitly or implicitly, to reject all heteronomous criteria for the interpretation of existence. How meaningful it is to talk of moral evil in this setting is difficult to say. One can, none the less, put forward the following points: that the phenomenology of these directors implies a moral attitude to reality, which they define in the rather negative sense of reaction against the established order; that in their films the structure of the existential situation itself

---

[1] A. Ayfre, *Dieu au cinéma* (Paris, 1953), ch. 4.
[2] I am giving names of directors and individuals and works purely as general orientation.

becomes the only guide for conduct; that reality understood in terms of experience easily becomes sufficient in itself and its own justification; and finally that what is "real" consequently boils down to what the director decides to accept as real.

Another aspect of their work is that their closeness to reality often loses its original motivation and becomes just a play of decorative images (not that this should be taken as denying the validity of other aspects of their work). Compare Bresson's treatment of temporality in *Un condamné à mort s'est échappé*, or Kurosawa's in *Living*, for example, with Alain Resnais's in *Last Year in Marienbad*; or a surrealist like Luis Buñuel's grasp of psychological truth (however debatable his works might be) with that of someone like Claude Lelouch as shown in *Un homme et une femme*.

II. THE WORLD BETWEEN LIGHT AND DARKNESS

It is not only the technical potential of the cinema that is a source of inspiration for today's directors. Many of them, the greatest of them certainly included, are working on what might be called the expressionism of the language of the cinema. This also involves moral reflection.

First, a general explanation. There has recently been a change in the way people look at the work of the cinema. While it was almost entirely an economic enterprise, the production of a film was controlled above all by the laws of return on capital invested and not by those of art. Under this regime, the director was in fact no more than an employee of the financial backers, who imposed their own conditions on him. Now, for various reasons, the situation has changed; the cinema (or at least a part of it) has become an art form, and the director has become a real "author". Cinema as a means of communication has changed from a technical medium indifferent to the object it was communicating to a specific organ of present-day culture putting across, in visual image and sound,[3] the world view of a particular person—the author-director. This is a key fact in interpreting the contemporary cinema: it means that the personality of the director will determine the character of the work, and that the

[3] E. Morin, *Le cinéma ou l'homme imaginaire* (Paris, 1956), p. 55.

expression "author" is applied not to a writer, but to a specialist in the art of making films.

The second of these two points implies that the idea of "author" (as opposed to the mere technical executive) is being used of someone who operates in the field of aesthetics. The author has become, in fact, an artist, and among the many shades of meaning that can be attached to the word "artist" the important one here is the idea of the artist as someone who has the capacity to exploit the technical means at his disposal to the maximum. So in the case of the figurative arts (including the cinema), the subject-matter can become a mere support for the creative intention behind it, which concentrates more on what the material used or the nature of the instruments used suggests to the imagination, so that the real meaning of the work comes to reside not in what it says but in the *way it says it*. The process can go even farther—the artist himself can become incapable of saying why he has chosen one particular form instead of another.

One of his reasons will be the different amount of rational or affective work required by the nature of each of the linguistic elements that make up the artist's means of expression. It is the task of the critic to try to clarify their influence and meaning. This is of prime importance here, since the fact that the directors mentioned choose a particular element of the cinematic language, and the use they make of it, show us certain aspects of their attitude to life that would otherwise remain hidden.

It would seem to be a useful exercise in critical orientation to undertake a brief historical survey, which must of necessity be the merest outline sketch. The history of the cinema shows good and evil confronting each other from two different points of view: either each is taken as an irreconcilable pole dividing humanity into "goodies" and "baddies" by reference to the law, or they are seen as indications of affective attitudes that imply a particular state of mind.

In the first case, once it has been decided whose side the law is on, the author has only to work things out so that the goodies win and order is restored out of chaos. This schema is inspired by an optimistic faith based on confidence in the security-giving magnanimity, justice and power of the rulers of the world, whoever they may be. This is the mould in which the classic Westerns are cast, as well as most detective and war films.

In the second, the author sees it as his task to create an "atmosphere" which, through its own quality, will induce the spectator to supply the feelings thought proper to a character dominated by good or evil, while relegating action to the back of the stage, a mere thematic link between atmospheres. This is the instinctive-emotional schema on which all the German expressionists of the 20's worked. To them can be added the names of Victor Sjöström and Carl Dreyer, whose works reproduce the mythical struggle between darkness and light. Unlike the first schema, this one is not based on understanding and control of causes (which remain obscure), but on purely affective description of their effects. Kracauer[4] has analysed the significance of such visions, by reference to the socio-psychological contexts of their authors, in a work that has become a classic.

In both cases, the authors start with a similar theme, the struggle between good and evil, but resolve the struggle along the lines best suited to their own inclinations, temperament and cultural context.

Looking at some recent productions in this light, one can pick out examples such as Alfred Hitchcock's *Psycho* and *The Birds*, Joseph Losey's *The Servant*, Ingmar Bergman's *The Seventh Seal*, *The Hour of the Wolf* and *Shame*, and Roman Polanski's *The Dance of the Vampires* and *Rosemary's Baby*, as films that stand out in this light as illustrations of the anguish felt by the greater part of humanity when faced with a feeling of imminent doom. In all these, man is shown as a victim of some *thing* that takes possession of him and drags him into either madness or death. The only far-off echo of hope to be heard is the proposal of love as the only force capable of redeeming life, of balancing or overcoming the disaster that has come or is to come.

It is not very difficult to see these images as illustrations of the spiritual climate of the world today. The characterization of the mental changes taking place today that I made at the beginning of this article can be applied here, with the note of euphoria in the discovery of authenticity somewhat muted and the inner

[4] S. Kracauer, *From Caligari to Hitler* (Princeton, 1947).

doubt and fear in the face of an uncertain future to the fore. For many people, reality has become less simple and more impenetrable in these last few years. Man has seen the collapse of many of the projects on which he set his hopes, and the unfolding of disconcerting horizons. Hence the increased interest in occultism and magic, indicative of the primitive sensation of being faced with a danger that cannot even be put into words and which therefore has to be exorcized in one way or another.

This is why these directors' vision of "reality" contains an element of terror beyond human control. Evil then comes to be seen not so much (or not only) as a quality of lower or weaker natures and not to be found in the well-born hero (the *simpliste* "goodies and baddies" first schema), but as a real, almost physical force, bent on destruction, which takes control of man and impedes his path to happiness and life (while not making it impossible, since his power of choice is still recognized). Another aspect of their representation of evil is that by relating it to sickly visions induced by madness or dreams, they set its presence and effect on the margin of moral and rational life, thereby making it difficult to define its real character and extent. Evil becomes a virus.

III. MORAL COMPROMISE OR AESTHETIC EVASION

The influential place occupied by cinema directors in today's culture prompts one more line of reflection. No one now denies the importance of the cinema. Television is making us even more accustomed to seeing and learning about the world in cinematic images. The director-author, for his part, is now conscious of the fact that his art has a meaning and is his vehicle in a dialogue with the whole world.

Looking back at the themes the cinema has dealt with on the basis of these premises, one can see that there are now important directors working who have made language—in the widest sense of the term—the subject of their work and thought. For some time this concentration on language takes the form of objective analysis of language and its artistic expression; for others that of the director questioning himself on his own loquacity.

A typical example of the first kind is Jean Luc Godard, who has made verbal ambiguity—the power of the word to clarify and obfuscate at the same time—the *leitmotif* of his entire work.[5] Into the same category would also come the Antonioni of *Blow-up*, Rohmer's *The Collector* and Lelouch's *Vivre pour vivre*, as examples of varying approaches to the theme. The most representative figure of the second school is undoubtedly Ingmar Bergman who, besides posing the theme of word and silence in his "trilogy",[6] has spelt out, from *Prison* to its culmination in *Persona*, a long, anguished meditation on the inner conflict of the artist who cannot reconcile his aesthetic life with his simply human life.

The interest these directors take in the phenomenon of language concerns us here, as does the compromise position they adopt in regard to it, to the extent that any posing of the problem of language entails a parallel posing of the problem of the theoretical-practical concept of truth and, in the final analysis, of what is real in the sense of being accessible to man. In other words, the artist's anxiety over the word is a reflection of his preoccupation with the old antinomy of appearances and what is truly real. And now his preoccupation is not that of an outside observer handing down judgments from a position of non-involvement, but that of someone who feels the difficulty in his own flesh, since what is in the balance is himself: his activity, his experiences, his convictions.

There is no space here for a fundamental examination of this attitude. The point is that these directors, living as they do in the tension of expressive endeavour, whose ideology will not admit a transcendent principle nor rely on the support of faith, find the world as it appears today somewhat lacking in meaning, and existence becoming inexplicable.[7] So it is not unusual for them to feel and express the agonizing sensation of walking on the edge of a precipice, and the terror of finding nothing but emptiness. This influences their moral schemas, built up on the

[5] Cf. the number of *Etudes cinématographiques* devoted to this director, 57/61 (Paris, 1967).

[6] *Idem* on Ingmar Bergman, 46/47 (Paris, 1966).

[7] I. Bergman, "La peau du serpent" (a presentation of *Persona*), in *Cahiers du cinéma*, 188 (Paris, 1967).

radical need for truth as a condition for survival and on the no less radically destructive nature of every form of falsehood.

From this, however, it does not necessarily follow that this affective attitude implies an equally radical search for truth and for the authentic meaning of existence. I would go further and say that, just as those who appeal to authenticity to cut reality down to size frequently find themselves ending up in empty formalism, so the artist placed in the compromising position of being forced to revise his conception of the universe can prefer to turn in on himself and seek refuge in aesthetic evasion. If this were to happen, there would then be a particular form of evil in the contemporary cinema: the evil of the abdication of the artist in the face of the need to remain faithful to his vocation and true to his destiny.

To sum up briefly: we can say that the contemporary cinema shares the tendencies that characterize our age; hence it knows what it rejects and leaves aside better than what it is searching for and ought to do.

With the exceptional cases of directors like Hitchcock, Bresson and Dreyer, it virtually unanimously describes a world closed to transcendence;[8] so it leaves out of account the Christian idea of sin, which supposes an acceptance of a transcendent order as a reference point for moral decision-making. In place of this it throws one back on one's own experience, accepted virtually without discrimination, progressively obscuring the outlines of what can be called "objectively evil".

By relating guilt to psychic and physical disorder, it projects evil over the entire universe, and through its purely immanentist interpretation of the world, seems to propose a moral-ontological view of reality constructed on the framework of a dualistic mystical philosophy.

[8] A. Ayfre, "L'ateismo nel cinema contemporaneo", in the encyclopedia *L'ateismo contemporaneo*, vol. I (Turin, 1968), p. 585.

Translated by Paul Burns

PART III
DOCUMENTATION
CONCILIUM

Concilium General Secretariat

Tempter and Temptation

ALL the articles in this issue centre upon the question of the reality of evil, and particularly on evil as a challenge to the Christian faith. The Christian message proclaims deliverance from evil.[1] When evil is felt gradually to lose its significance as a reality, there will be less interest in being delivered from it.[2]

As man becomes more conscious of his autonomy, he will take the fight against evil into his own hands, both in the world at large (for example, preventing war by the systematic organization of peace, or combating racial discrimination) and at the personal level (for example, a scientific promotion of mental health).

In this perspective the cessation of evil would be simply a matter of time and of scientific awareness. This sober attitude towards evil has shed much light on the obscure reality which philosophy and theology have tried to comprehend for centuries.

On the other hand, in our own time new evils are constantly being introduced into society. Is this a kind of inevitable fate? Has evil a kind of inherent fertility by which it propagates itself

[1] For recent literature, particularly about the point of contact between sociology and ethics, cf. M. D. Chenu, O. H. Pesch, C. Gerest, F. X. Kaufmann, J. M. Pohier, P. Bourgy, "Loi et Evangile", in *La Vie Spir.* (Supp.), 90 (Sept. 1969), pp. 287–365; Pesch's article appeared, in an expanded form, in his "Gesetz und Evangelium. Luthers Lehre im Blick auf das moraltheologische Problem des ethischen Normenzerfalls", in *Theol. Quartalschr.*, 149, 4 (1969), pp. 313–45.

[2] V. Fagone's "Coscienza morale e trasformazione scientifica del mondo" discusses the prospects of the American Academy of Arts and Sciences for the year 2000, under the leadership of D. Bell, in *La Civiltà Cattolica*, 121 (3 Jan. 1970, no. 2869), pp. 32–46.

and which we can never eradicate? Should it be put down to the fact that man is finite and deficient?

These questions are constantly asked when people talk about the evil they experience.[3] We could get over these problems if man could achieve perfect autonomy and put himself beyond good and evil. Nietzsche tried to work this out on the ground that Western man[4] in the past concentrated exclusively on reason and will—particularly the deliberate will to power—and so put humanity in a situation of underdevelopment.

This belief in man's ability to cross the frontier between good and evil has not prevented man from being daily confronted with the reality of evil, particularly in the structures of power. It is therefore not astonishing that reflection on the inevitable reality of evil has led to new approaches in both philosophy and theology.

In this situation the question of man's responsibility for evil inevitably crops up again.[5] When man has become conscious that he is in charge of existence, he will also be ready to assume responsibility for what is happening to this existence. Doesn't he overrate himself when he assumes all responsibility? Throughout the centuries this question has always prompted another one, that of the tempter and temptation.

The recognition that evil is larger than man leads either to the acceptance of some kind of fatalism, to the acceptance of evil as an autonomous principle, or it makes man look into this experience of his, and examine his awareness of a process within human responsibility, which he describes as temptation. But temptation would seem to imply a tempter.

This awareness has found expression in a multiplicity of myths where the tempter is described with a rich variety of names.

[3] J. Hick, "God, Evil and Mystery", in *Religious Studies*, 3, nos. 1 and 2 (1968), pp. 539–46; Haig Khatchadourian, "God, Happiness and Evil", *ibid.*, 2, nos. 1 and 2 (1967), pp. 109–19.

[4] Cf. F. de Smaele, "Aspecten van de ethische problematiek" (with a French abstract: "Quelques aspects d'une problématique de la morale"), in *Tijdschr. v. Filosofie* (June 1967), pp. 203–60.

[5] J. D. Stewart, "Paul Ricoeur's Phenomenology of Evil", in *Intern. Philos. Quarterly*, 9, no. 4 (Dec. 1969), pp. 573–89); R. A. McCormick, "Notes on Moral Theology", in *Theological Studies*, 30, no. 4 (Dec. 1969), esp. pp. 668–80; A. Uleyn, *Is it I, Lord? Pastoral Psychology and the Recognition of Guilt* (New York, 1969).

Christianity described this process in terms of temptation by the devil, a theme with many variations in Christian literature.

In this literature the tempter-figures of Faust, Don Juan and such female counterparts as Celestina, have become classics of their kind. Today the theme plays such a significant part in the theatre (for example, in Dürrenmatt's *Don Juan und die Liebe zur Mathematik*), in films[6] (e.g., in *Rosemary's Baby*) and in literature (as in Julien Green's *Moira*), that it is clear that modern man sees in it something corresponding to his own experience.

The same is true of Picasso's work, which shows evil as irresistible. That the artist shows the truth through a lie has become a proverbial paradox. This holds also when the artist develops the story of temptation and the tempter in his own way. The story may be mythical, and no longer agree with our rational interpretation, but it still makes us think.

The myth can no longer stand up to such questions as: Does the devil really exist? or: Must we believe in the existence of Satan?—and so on.[7] But the questions are probably wrongly put. The real question might be: Does this primitive story tell us something that could shed some light on the dark side of man's existence? Is the nature of man's responsibility for the evil introduced into this world such that it assumes its full tragic significance only when human awareness accepts this area of temptation without allowing it to alienate him from his own humanity?[8]

When we examine recent work by biblical scholars, philosophers and theologians, this seems to be a point of convergence: in man's responsibility for evil there is a margin of temptation which does not make a tempter superfluous nor the forgiveness

---

[6] Apart from the contributions in this issue, cf. A. Hertz, "Religionskritik im Film—Überlegungen eines Theologen", in *Stimmen der Zeit*, 95 (March 1970), pp. 180-7; F. Dürrenmatt, "Theaterprobleme", in *Theater-Schriften und Reden* (Zürich, 1966), pp. 92-131; P. Berrigan, "Hell is Other People", in *Continuum*, 6 (Oct. 1968), pp. 414-7; H. P. Madler, "Dürrenmatts mutiger Mensch", in *Hochland*, 62 (Jan./Feb. 1970), pp. 36-49.

[7] E. Rideau, "Essai sur le langage de la foi", in *Nouv. Rev. Théol.*, 101 (Dec. 1969), pp. 1045-72; D. M. Rasmussen, "Ricoeur: the Anthropological Necessity of a Special Language", in *Continuum*, 7 (Feb./May 1969), pp. 120-30.

[8] C. Curran, "Social Ethics and Method in Moral Theology", *ibid.*, pp. 50-62.

of man's failure and guilt so obvious as to be superficial. In other words, the question of redemption can again be reasonably put, however modestly.

Apart from biblical scholarship, philosophy and theology, other disciplines have shed some light on this complex obscurity of temptation and guilt; but we shall limit ourselves to these three lines of investigation.

1. The Contribution of Exegesis

A first point that has been established by modern exegesis[9] is that the identification of the tempter with Satan, the devil, Beelzebub and so on, appears only in the later books of the Bible. The way in which these names are taken for granted goes back to the linguistic usage of the cultures that surrounded Israel, rather than to the religious conviction of the authors.

It is asking too much of Scripture when one tries to find there an explanation of how far such personifications of the tempter should be taken as real: "In the days of Jesus the existence of demons was taken for granted. It is nevertheless to the point to remember that the Old Testament practically never speaks of them (only Tobias mentions them, as far as I know) and that they are therefore a rather late feature."[10]

Western man, with his ontological mentality, will perhaps too easily conclude that the devil does not exist. But the biblical scholar cannot put the question aside so glibly: "Jesus does not simply expel demons, but frees people from the (supposed) power of the demons. And though these demons have no objective reality

[9] For bibliography see J. Dupont, "L'origine du récit des tentations de Jésus au désert", in Rev. Biblique, 73 (1966), pp. 30–76; L. Randellini, "Satana nell' Antiquo Testamento", in Biblia e Oriente, 5 (1963), pp. 123–32; A. M. Dubarle, "La tentation diabolique dans le Livre de la Sagesse", in Mélanges Tisserant, I (Città del Vaticano, 1964), pp. 187–95; B. Gerhardson, The Testing of God's Son (Lund, 1966); H. Clavier, "Tentation et 'Anamartésie' dans le Nouveau Testament", in Rev. d'Hist. et de Phil. Rel., 47 (1967), pp. 151–64; J. Navone, "The Temptation Account in St Luke 4. 1–13", in Scripture, 20 (1968), pp. 65–72; J. F. Braghan, "The Gerasene Demoniac", in Cath. Bibl. Qu., 30, 4 (1968), pp. 522–36; P. Lamarche, "Le possédé de Gérasa", in Nouv. Rev. Théol., 90, 6 (1968), pp. 581–97; B. van Iersel, "Jezus, duivel en demonen", in Engelen en duivels (Hilversum, 1967), pp. 5–22 and 91–4.

[10] B. van Iersel, loc. cit., p. 97.

where we are concerned, the liberation and redemption of these people is real, even if we no longer describe the evil from which they are delivered as 'demons' or 'unclean spirits'."[11]

Scripture puts the universal human experience of liability to evil, of being tempted by something or somebody stronger than man, in the perspective of redemption. Man may rely on the message of redemption for his well-founded hope that this menace, too, will not prevent his ultimate deliverance. The seriousness with which one listens to and accepts the message of redemption also determines the seriousness of what one believes one is redeemed from.

A second point is found in what exegetes like Schlier[12] have to say about the powers and forces which the New Testament presents as overcome by Christ, particularly in the Pauline writings. These positive assertions and statements of the New Testament cannot be disposed of simply by referring the powers and forces to a mythical picture of the world. Man is indeed threatened by forces outside himself, by situations beyond his control, by the menacing character of the whole of reality, experienced by man as meaningless and leading only to death.[13]

The biblical message reveals no new realities which fill man with anxiety and are therefore likely to paralyse his development. Anxiety and despair exist, and within this sphere man is given the encouraging message of a grace that is stronger than evil.

The contribution of the biblical scholars lies mainly in that they have made it possible for modern man, too, to understand the message and indeed the necessity of salvation on the ground of the menaces that beset us today.

How to translate this message into Christian practice is another question. In any case, it does not do justice to the message of the Bible to see it simply as an exercise in exorcism (mythical magic), or as simply telling us to ignore Satan and the powers as the superfluous remnants of a culture that has been left behind. To do this would simply be to belittle the seriousness of evil, contrary to our experience of it.

[11] Id., ibid., p. 98.
[12] Mächte und Gewalten im Neuen Testament (Quaest. Disp. 3, Freiburg i. Br., 1958), p. 13.   [13] Op. cit., pp. 26-8 and 50-63.

A third exegetical contribution mainly concerns the theologians, although biblical scholars admit that the texts have not yet been completely and satisfactorily analysed. It is very clear to the theologians that there are no elements in the scriptural message which allow of a kind of demonology in its own right.[14] Whatever Scripture says about temptation, devil and powers of evil occurs in the margin of the real biblical message, and these elements are better integrated in the context of a modern ethics than given an independent vague and gnostic existence in separate treatises on the devil.

2. Philosophical Considerations

The results of psychoanalytic thought and of the macro-structure of evil which, particularly after World War II, was experienced as a basic threat to humanity (concentration camps, discrimination, underdevelopment, the alienation created by structures), has led thinkers, particularly those described as reflective philosophers,[15] to reconsider the whole problem of evil.

There is no room here for even a mere outline of the way in which Kant's separation of pure knowledge from morality (reine Vernunft from praktische Vernunft) has again to be bridged today. Suffice to say that today even the most ferocious protagonist of the so-called exact sciences can no longer maintain that there is a science without values. Every scientific progress contains moral implications. One has but to think of the splitting of the atom, the penetration of biology into the secrets of life, and the possibilities of manipulating the origin of man as a human being.

Some make a certain exception with regard to this detachment from values for a tendency in psychoanalysis which sees itself as a kind of physical science of the mind and seems to have inherited the kind of determinism which, in a different form, is reappearing in structuralism[16] and new forms of behaviourism. Other

[14] A. Winklhofer, Traktat über den Teufel (Frankfurt a. M., 1961) and the 1948 issue of Etudes Carmélitaines on this topic both tend in this direction. Cf. an art. by C. Moeller on the ambiguity of Satan in Coll. Mechlin. (1949), pp. 191–203; K. Rahner, "Dämonologie", in Lex. f. Theol. u. Kirche, 3 (Freiburg, 1959), cols. 145–7; C. Duquoc, "Symbole ou réalité?", in Lumière et Vie, 14, 78 (May/Aug. 1966), pp. 99–105.

[15] L. Lacroix, Panorama de la philosophie française contemporaine (Paris, 1966), pp. 15–23 and 38–47.

[16] M. Foucault, Les mots et les choses. Une archéologie des sciences

articles in this issue have shown that it would be unfair to blame Freud for such a unilateral interpretation of the psyche as a kind of natural object, working on its own principles, principles which we can then discover separately.

Those philosophers who pursue the reflective method accepted the evidence provided by psychoanalysis on the one hand, and comparative religion on the other, but it is to their credit that, instead of taking those data as definitive, they used them as bases for further development.[17]

It would seem obvious, for instance, that, in so far as culpability is concerned, psychoanalysis cannot go beyond the feeling of guilt, or, with regard to temptation, the feeling of being tempted. But feelings of guilt are usually misleading because they reveal more about somebody's ideals than about his actual ethical disposition.

The same applies to the feeling of being tempted: it reflects more an escape from responsibility than the actual point where man has lapsed. We see this in the mythical stories[18] where the tempter is endowed with a half human and a half supra-human shape. They can easily alienate man from his own responsibility and make him shift the blame for his lapse on to something or somebody else, whether we call this Satan, environment, structure, public opinion, indoctrination or whatever. It always shows the pattern of alienation: the other is to blame.

The experience of those feelings and mythical stories may, however, have a deeper sense. And this deeper sense cannot be taken for granted, but has to be looked for at the level of rationality. It is the philosopher's function to bring the phenomena within the sphere of reason and to extract the meaning. In this sense

---

humaines (Paris, 1966); M. Corvez, "Le structuralisme de Jacques Lacan", in Rev. Phil. de Louvain, 66 (May 1968), pp. 282–308; A. Fialkowski, "Structuralisme et herméneutique", in Esprit, 34, nos. 7 and 8 (1966), pp. 16–30; A. M. Tronos, "El hombre y su lenguaje", in Razón y Fe, 178 (July/Aug. 1968), pp. 59–78; P. Valori, "Strutturalismo e morale", in La Civiltà Cattolica, 118 (Dec. 1967), pp. 422–34.

[17] P. Ricoeur, De l'interprétation. Essai sur Freud (Paris, 1965); id., "La psychanalyse et le mouvement de la culture contemporaine', in S. Nacht, Traité de psychanalyse (Paris, 1965), pp. 79–109.

[18] R. Pattazzoni, Myths of Beginning and Creation Myths. Essay on the History of Religion (Leiden, 1954), p. 26.

Ricoeur summed up his outstanding examination of the myth[19] in the terse phrase: "The myth sets us thinking."

For this reason, Ricoeur also accepts Freud, so carefully avoided by both philosophers and theologians under the pretext that he had been disposed of, as somebody who makes us think afresh about, among other things, that most interiorized form of evil, the feeling of guilt. The psychoanalyst will probably interpret the strange phenomenon that psychoanalysis is absent from practically all theological and philosophical studies on hermeneutics as a form of narcissism or repression.

Freud himself frequently called what he tried to do *Deutungskunst*, the art of interpretation, an ability which demands much tact and practice. One can, though not without difficulty, draw up strict rules for this and it can be made to rest on a most coherent system of rules and regulations.

What has sometimes been called, in line with the Copernican revolution and Darwin's thesis of evolution, the Freudian discovery, was formulated by Freud himself in the meaningful submission that the ego is not master in his own house.

This ego has inevitably succumbed to the temptation of language[20] and can only exist if it surrenders to that language. In this context an English author has made the interesting observation that in our age Satan, the tempter, must be identified with language.[21]

In the story man tells about himself and what surrounds him, he always uses a language which he has not created himself, so that he always and necessarily uses phrases and fragments of an already existing story. Words like "I", "man", "god", "identity", "distinction", "contradiction", "reality", and so on, undoubtedly belong to these fragments.

The refusal to subject oneself to language, to function as a character in a story, to take up and recognize this story, means that

---

[19] *Finitude et culpabilité. II. La symbolique du Mal* (Paris, 1960).

[20] S. Ijsseling, "Paul Ricoeur en Sigmund Freud" (French summary), in *Tijdschr. v. Fil.*, 30 (1968), pp. 695–714.

[21] E. Gellner, "The Devil in Modern Philosophy", in *The Hibbert Journal*, 56 (Oct./July 1958), p. 253; cf. J. Derrida: "The external evil... lies at the heart of the living word as the principle of its effacement", quoted by H. Parret, "Jacques Derrida. Een wijsbegeerte van de Schriftuur", in *Tijdschr. v. Fil.*, 30 (1968), p. 67.

the person locks himself inside himself and becomes totally un-intelligible. To live by a statute other than that which governs what is spoken about, who is spoken to, and the speaker, is the most profound form of alienation.

This is but an example to explain why the story man tells about himself in the myth,[22] or repeats in psychoanalysis, also sets the philosopher thinking, and the theologian as well when he reads for a second time a story he thought he had already understood.

Both temptation and tempter occur in the story of the myth as in that of psychoanalysis, but this does not do away with culpability. A curious paradox is maintained throughout: man is responsible for the existing evil although he inevitably yields to temptation. One would rather think that temptation would suspend or obstruct responsibility or that it would make the tempter responsible for the evil that is inevitably introduced into this world in this way. The philosopher is surprised that neither the myth nor psychoanalysis[23] draws this conclusion.

This leads the philosopher to examine whether and how the myth tells us something original about evil and temptation; whether and how psychoanalysis penetrates into the human *arche* (origin), the beginning of evil and temptation in the region where reason is silent.

In his carefully argued investigation, Ricoeur brought this story of evil and temptation back into the region of rationality.[24] In this way he managed to pull evil out of the blind alley of ontology (evil is non-being, or evil is something of its own with its own creator, a kind of anti-god), and to place it again in the context of man's experience of freedom.

In exercising his freedom, man creates for himself the possibility of being himself: a *cogito* (I think). The morally good and morally evil must be ascribed to this *cogito*. Ethically man opts

[22] A. Vergote: "... The myth is purely man, not a vision of the world, but the discourse of the Other who manifests the world and reveals man to himself.... The myth is not the word of man speaking about things, but the prior language which happens to man and allows him to speak about things", in "Mythe, croyance aliénée et foi théologale", in *Mythe et Foi* (Paris, 1966), pp. 164–6.

[23] A. Caracciolo, "Le mal dans l'expérience religieuse", in *Le mythe de la peine* (Paris, 1967), pp. 265–74.

[24] *Op. cit.*, II, and "Interprétation du mythe de la peine", in *op. cit.*, pp. 23–42.

for this freedom but in this very option already admits his limitation. He is conscious of being able to do more and better, but he must opt for his limitations precisely in order to be a conscious *cogito*. And so he already yields to the unavoidable temptation to co-operate with what Nabert[25] has called "the division of consciousnesses" (*séparation des consciences*).

This temptation can hardly be personified as a reality outside man, but is no less real for that. This argument of reflective philosophy leads Peperzak to conclude: "It seems to me that if Satan has any meaning at all he is an apparent contradiction in creation, which in turn leads to the problem whether in fact everything has been created."[26]

In this last remark we still find an echo of that worry of all classical theodicy: if evil exists in its own right, God, the creator of all, must be the cause of it. Here we discover traces of that temptation to postulate another principle of evil, subject to God the creator: a force which counteracts God—a way of thinking which is not wholly absent from some of the names given to the tempter in the Bible.

Peperzak continues: "From the philosophical point of view it seems to me that the question concerning something like Satan is very important. But if we are going to talk about it, we shall have to look for some way of translating the word, and in philosophy I would then find a kind of parallel in meaninglessness, or in the apparent or threatening meaninglessness which we find in evil as a kind of puzzle or question-mark when we think about it. . . . The origin of meaninglessness is precisely what I experience as preceding the fact that I in all freedom co-operate with it."[27]

Authors like Bataille, Réage and Genet feature a very different kind of temptation to evil,[28] more on the lines of de Sade: evil is deliberately chosen as an anti-pattern and an anti-value, or, as Rahner put it,[29] a kind of mystique of sin. Evil is then radically

---

[25] J. Nabert, *Essai sur le mal* (Paris, 1955), pp. 86–7: "What the feeling of sin warns us against is a complacency of the self about the self, by which the self excludes itself from all communication with other beings"; and p. 111: "The one is in us, as pure consciousness is in the 'I'."

[26] *Engelen en duivels, loc. cit.*, p. 105.   [27] *Op. cit.*, p. 106.

[28] F. de Smaele, *loc. cit.*, p. 233.

[29] "Situationsethik und Sündenmystik", in *Stimmen der Zeit*, 145 (1950), pp. 330–42.

chosen as a privileged access to the holy. Basically this seems to approach Nietzsche's view of transcending both evil and goodness.

Nabert's approach to the problem is more serious.[30] He finds the density of evil so insoluble that, though he is not a Christian philosopher, he wonders whether this evil does not postulate a transcendent Forgiver, or whether, with Sartre, we must admit that existence is basically meaningless and man is doomed to fall victim to the temptation of the meaningless.

3. The Challenge to Theology

If the philosopher is forced, on re-reading the myth concerned with guilt and the story that man tells about himself in psychoanalysis, to rethink the problem of guilt and temptation, the results of some trends in modern philosophy in turn constitute a challenge to theology. For theology cannot afford to ignore a reality which tradition, however poorly, has indicated with a multiplicity of names.[31]

Such a theological reflection is not bound to give pride of place to the question whether the tempter has an autonomous, objective existence of his own, distinct from human existence, as a pure spirit.[32] Such considerations indeed lead too easily to an independent treatment of the subject in separate demonologies,[33] which contort the perspective.

Rahner[34] wonders whether we do not too glibly reject purely spiritual beings, even though it is certain that they do not directly belong to the subject-matter of revelation. What revelation says

[30] J. Nabert, Le désir de Dieu (Paris, 1966), a posthumous work with a preface by P. Ricoeur: "To this unjustifiable element corresponds a desire for justification which conforms to no rules. Since ethics is inadequate, we have to turn to religious experience."

[31] J. Quinlan, "Engelen en duivels", in Tijdschr. v. Theol., 7 (1967), pp. 43–62; F. Gokey, The Terminology for the Devil and Evil Spirits in the Apostolic Fathers (Washington, 1961); B. Kelly, God, Men and Satan (Dublin, 1950).

[32] P. Schoonenberg, "Wijsgerige en theologische opmerkingen over engelen en duivelen", in Engelen en duivels, pp. 66–90, and the discussion between Schoonenberg and Peperzak, ibid., pp. 10–107.

[33] Cf. note 14.

[34] "Theologisches zum Monogenismus", in Schriften zur Theologie, I (Einsiedeln, 1956), pp. 253–322, specially p. 320.

about them is always in reference to man and the human condition.

We can formulate the point negatively by saying that, whenever the assumption of a tempter's existence destroys or diminishes man's responsibility for evil, it necessarily impairs the message of redemption.

Positively speaking, we must say that, where the Churches have forgotten their exorcizing mission today, they fail in their function. When, in earlier centuries, the Church exorcized the *daimones*, the demons, it expressed what Paul mentioned as an aspect of Christian redemption: that our struggle is not with flesh and blood but with powers. Harvey Cox,[35] who frankly favours demythologization, nevertheless refers to the need for a new ecclesial exorcism, now that those demons are called public opinion, militarism, capitalism, pan-sexualism, racial discrimination, productiveness, consumption and so on.[36]

People must be brought back from their enchantment by other worlds, astrological, metaphysical or religious, and urged to face the concrete value of this one world, "where alone the true call of God can be understood". They must be delivered from the stupefying fads which give them a false view of social realities, and from the active and negative patterns of behaviour that result from these illusions.

While this may not yet be as clear as one might think, it is possible that the theologians of social criticism, of *Kritischer Katholizismus* and *Tegenspraak*,[37] will point out new concrete evidence of this temptation in the structures and concentrations of power which they want to break down.

Although this struggle is not against a personal devil, it is no less serious or important. Even though the seriousness of the faith

---

[35] *The Secular City* (London, 1967), pp. 193 ff.
[36] P. Thibaud, "Consommateurs, sauvons-nous nous-mêmes"; P. Kende, "Mythes et réalités de la 'société de consommation' "; J. M. Domenach, "Critique d'un éloge", in *Esprit*, 37, n. 387 (Dec. 1969), pp. 842–83: "Dépasser la société de consommation".
[37] A. Fabry, "De industriële samenleving repressief en konfidentiëel", in *Tegenspraak*, 1, 3 (1970), pp. 55–64; "De funktie van het christendom in het laatkapitalisme", *ibid.*, pp. 38–54; V. Fagone, "Coscienza morale e trasformazione scientifica del mondo", in *Civiltà Catt.*, 121, 2869 (3 Jan. 1970), pp. 32–47.

would reduce the tempter to the situation in which we live and which we have chosen, we cannot simply accept that situation as mere fatality.

This is in line with a conviction which is certainly part and parcel of the Christian achievement, namely, that man is responsible also for the evil that is or appears greater than himself: evil as the result of human mismanagement. For the Christian, evil is not something to be discarded as a negligible waste of the good, or as neutral results of social structures and psychological dispositions.

On the other hand, it has always been the conviction of the Church that this responsibility for evil is not disposed of by the belief that man is tempted, and that he yields to evil. This creates for pastoral theology the difficult problem of how evil can be effectively forgiven.

It is clear that, as Bonhoeffer says, cheap forgiveness does not do justice to the seriousness of evil and temptation: "Cheap grace is the arch-enemy of our Church: grace that costs man nothing, justification of sin, grace without imitation, without cross, without Christ". On the other hand, precisely the automation and registration of human failures by computers and data-banks reduce the effectiveness of ecclesial forgiveness. It is hoped that soon a special issue of *Concilium* will be devoted to this problem in all its complexity.[38]

[38] The *Dogma* issue for 1971.

Translated by Theo Westow

Biographical Notes

Louis Beirnaert, s.j., born 2 April 1906 in France, ordained in 1937. He studied at the Catholic Faculties at Lille and the Gregorian in Rome. He holds a licentiate in letters and in theology, and teaches theology at the Jesuit theological faculty at Enghien in France. He is also a psychoanalyst and the editor of the journal *Études*. His published works include *Expérience chrétienne et Psychologie* (Paris, 1966).

Thomas Berry, c.p., born 9 November 1914 in the U.S.A., ordained 1942. He studied at the Catholic University of America. He holds a doctorate in history (1949) and teaches the history of religions at Fordham University in the United States. His published works include *Buddhism* (New York, 1967).

José Luis Duhourq, born 15 November 1929 in Buenos Aires, ordained in 1954. He studied at the University of Paris and at the Gregorian in Rome. He holds licentiates in philosophy, theology and letters (art and archaeology), is Vice-Rector of the Great seminary in Buenos Aires and teaches aesthetics at the University of Salvador in Argentina.

Fergus Kerr, o.p., born 16 July 1931 in Scotland, ordained 1962. He studied in Scotland at the University of Aberdeen, at Oxford, at Le Saulchoir and at Munich. He holds an M.A. and a further degree in theology and teaches at the Dominican house in Oxford. He has published various articles in *New Blackfriars* and *Slant*.

Wilhelm Korff, born 29 November 1926 in Germany, ordained 1952. He studied at the University of Bonn. He at one time taught fundamental theology at the University of Münster and at present is preparing for his *habilitation* in theology. His published works include *Ehre, Prestige, Gewissen* (Cologne, 1966).

Wolf-Dieter Marsch, born 2 October 1928 in Germany. He is a member of the Evangelical Church. He studied in Germany at Greifswald, Tübingen and Göttingen and in the United States at Nashville. He holds a master's degree and doctorate in theology (1957) and teaches at the senior ecclesiastical school in Wuppertal-Barmen in Germany. His published works include *Gegenwart Christi in der Gesellschaft* (Munich, 1965) and *Hoffen worauf?* (Hamburg, 1963).

JACQUES-MARIE POHIER, O.P., born 23 August 1926 in France, ordained 1954. He studied in France at the Sorbonne and at the theological and philosophical faculties of Le Saulchoir, and in Canada at the University of Montreal. He holds a licentiate in theology and a doctorate in philosophy (1959) and is Vice-Rector of the Faculties at Le Saulchoir, where he is also honorary professor. His published works include *Psychologie et Théologie* (Paris, 1967).

WERNER POST, born 28 January 1940 in Germany. He is a Roman Catholic. He holds a doctorate in philosophy (1968) and is doing research in philosophy at the Senior Pedagogical School in Bonn. He contributed articles to *Sacramentum Mundi*: "Anthropomorphism", "Persecution of Christians", "Ideology", "Marxism" and "Scepticism".

PAUL RICOEUR, born 27 February 1913 in France. He studied at the Universities of Rennes and Paris. He is *agrégé* in philosophy, holds a doctorate in letters (1950), and is head of the Humanities faculty at Paris-Nanterre. His published works include *Philosophie de la volonté*, of which three volumes have so far appeared: *Le volontaire et l'involontaire* (Paris, 1950), *Finitude et culpabilité: 1. L'homme faillible; 2. La symbolique du mal* (Paris, 1960), and *De l'interprétation. Essai sur Freud* (Paris, 1965). He is a member of the editorial committee of the journal *Esprit*.

NORBERT SCHIFFERS, born 14 June 1926 in Germany, ordained 1952. He studied at the University of Tübingen. He holds a doctorate in theology (1954), passed his *habilitation* in 1968, and teaches fundamental theology at the University of Regensburg in Germany. His published works include *Einheit der Kirche* (Düsseldorf, 1956) and *Fragen der Physik an die Theologie* (Düsseldorf, 1968).

International Publishers of CONCILIUM

ENGLISH EDITION
Herder and Herder, Inc.
New York, U.S.A.

Burns & Oates Ltd.
25 Ashley Place
London, S.W.1

DUTCH EDITION
Uitgeverij Paul Brand, N.V.
Hilversum, Netherlands

FRENCH EDITION
Maison Mame
Tours/Paris, France

JAPANESE EDITION (PARTIAL)
Nansôsha
Tokyo, Japan

GERMAN EDITION
Verlagsanstalt Benziger & Co., A.G.
Einsiedeln, Switzerland

Matthias Grunewald-Verlag
Mainz, W. Germany

SPANISH EDITION
Ediciones Cristianidad
Salamanca, Spain

PORTUGUESE EDITION
Livraria Morais Editoria, Ltda.
Lisbon, Portugal

ITALIAN EDITION
Editrice Queriniana
Brescia, Italy

POLISH EDITION (PARTIAL)
Pallottinum
Poznań, Poland